P9-CRL-558

PERFECT
palette

PERFECT
palettes

Inspirational Color
Schemes for the
Home Decorator

STEPHANIE HOPPEN
text by Joanna Copestick

Clarkson Potter/Publishers
New York

Published in the United States by Clarkson Potter/Publishers,
an imprint of the Crown Publishing Group, a division of
Random House, Inc., New York.

www.crownpublishing.com
www.clarksonpotter.com

CLARKSON POTTER is a trademark and POTTER with
colophon is a registered trademark of Random House, Inc.

Published in Great Britain by Jacqui Small LLP, London.

Library of Congress Cataloging-in-Publication Data is
available upon request.

ISBN 978-0-307-46178-0

Printed in Singapore

10 9 8 7 6 5 4 3 2 1

First U.S. Edition

CONTENTS

inspired by color

I've always been excited about the ways in which color can be employed to transform a space, whether it is in the form of pictures, paint or wallpaper, furniture or fabric.

The glorious thing about color is the abundance of energy and emotion it brings to a space, whether a relaxing, cappuccino-toned living room or a smart, enlivening burgundy-inspired dining space. From cool hues and pale off-whites to rich cyclamen pinks and life-enhancing leaf greens, this book is about making color work, taking inspiration from key designers and their personal color philosophy, and applying color knowledge to every room in the home. Color is making a comeback. The long love affair with everything pale and neutral is not over, but new tones of subtle color are now being suffused with the old favorites to create clean, bright warming spaces.

Everyone has their own unique sense of color, derived from all kinds of sources. Favorite colors may be a result of well-remembered places or things from childhood, a special item of clothing, a treasured object, or a particular place such as a comfortable kitchen.

Often responses to the world around us are formed from perceived colors—the joy of a seascape, the fascinating tonal variations found in

OPPOSITE Hilton McConnico's Paris apartment is a virtuoso study in cool eau-de-nil, complementary reds, and analogous lilacs and purples, with a wall of mirror rather than a wall of color that serves to reflect all the tones back into the space.

a forest in the fall, or a perfect plate of complementary tomato and basil salad. These winning combinations can sometimes be transposed as color schemes to rooms with great effect; others may need toning down to achieve a similarly pleasing emotional response.

Walking into a room where the color is right is akin to enjoying a perfectly balanced meal or listening to uplifting music—a sensory delight, mood-enhancing, and satisfying to linger in. Color, elegantly handled, is as important as a carefully chosen piece of furniture or a well laid-out room in creating a home. It is a vital component in making a space feel alive and welcoming.

Designing with color is all about choosing what feels right for you, choosing a palette you will want to live with. If your wardrobe is packed with blue clothes, the chances are you will also be drawn to blues and similar tones when it comes to decorating your home.

Getting color right calls for some intuition, a few basic rules for combining colors, and an understanding of how colors work, together and alone. This book explains the properties, performances, and personalities of different colors, and shows how to look at color, assesses why it works, and provides dozens of palette choices and variations across the color spectrum, from warm pink and active green to cool neutral oatmeal and seductive eggplant. Now go paint!

working
with color

GETTING COLOR RIGHT

ABOVE New York-based designer Jamie Drake has created layers of mellow yellow for this bedroom, in which animal print furnishings are right at home against walls that evoke a hot African sun.

RIGHT Soft broken color applied in a wash to the walls provides ample texture in a light and airy bedroom, designed by Karl Fournier and Olivier Marty of Studio KO. The only additional color needed is added in the drapes, in the form of deep purple, to emphasize the subtle pink pigment on the walls.

COLOR IS A VITAL TOOL FOR CREATING SUCCESSFUL INTERIORS, AND WHETHER IT IS USED IN STRONG TONES OF GENEROUS PROPORTIONS OR AS A SUBTLE BACKDROP TO SMALLER JOLTS OF COLOR, IT IS VERY OFTEN THE COLOR THAT FIRST STRIKES YOU ON ENTERING A ROOM.

The new colors that excite me are the interesting, muted but elegant tones that bring warmth and energy to a space. Shades such as steely hibiscus blues, muted French grays, ultra-chic celery, and delicate alabaster. And there are strong tones too, such as full-on fuchsia, rich, deep eggplant, and dark, dramatic periwinkle. Plus, of course, the perfect white—panna cotta if you will—which is not white at all, but rather a mix of white with hints of other hues to "dirty" it up and create the impression of a neutral backdrop.

These inspiring colors are all around us, in nature, food, art, and architecture, from Rajasthan to Reykjavik, Florida to Florence. They are a mix of the contemporary and the comfortable, understated but inspiring, delicate but not elusive, strong but not overpowering. Color is one of life's great luxuries—it is inspiring to work with and extremely satisfying to live with when you get it right. Creating palettes of harmonious tones or complementary shades is an uplifting and invigorating process, just the thing for re-energizing interiors and creating a whole new atmosphere for a room.

The application of scientific theory to choosing colors for the home has some value, but it should not dictate hard and fast rules when it comes to choosing perfect palettes. Color wheels and color saturation charts can confound more than inspire; I find I work with color on an instinctive basis. It is of course useful and necessary to have an awareness of which colors work naturally with or complement one another, but often it is how a color makes you feel that will be a starting point in a room. We've all seen color mistakes, where all-pervasive shades that jar the senses have been misguidedly seen as "taking a bold approach," or where the dreaded magnolia has been employed solely as a "safe" option.

It has been inspiring talking to some of the most inventive paint makers and designers around to find out why they make and use the paint they do. Francesca Wezel of Francesca's Paints draws her inspiration from years of travel to exotic locations, while David Oliver of the Paint Library takes an almost scholarly approach to selecting and refining a unique palette of perfect off-whites. In New York Jamie Drake is unique in his use of vivid colors, from sunshine yellow to primary pink, and French designer Agnès Emery employs a range of rich blues, greens, and yellows in her colorful interiors that are full of multi-colored tiles and saturated hues.

Those designers noted for their innate sense of color, such as Tara Bernard, often go beyond the confines of pure color theory, mixing and matching tones and hues of the same color band as much as they do distinct colors.

TOP LEFT A nautical country palette in a Cornish dining room calls for the traditional creamware combination of powder blue and clotted cream for its seaside inspiration.

TOP RIGHT Pink can work as a wall color if it is kept towards the red or salmon end of the spectrum, so it doesn't stray into baby pink territory.

BOTTOM LEFT This glorious, light-filled coastal home by Jane Churchill is a white-on-white story offset by lime-colored cushions, deep green topiaries, and delicate off-white upholstery. Simply charming.

BOTTOM RIGHT Various shades of green are a good substitute for a treescape in this children's room in a New York urban apartment. Green often works best when used in a combination of shades rather than as a blanket approach.

HOW COLOR WORKS

"Color is the simplest and most obvious defining element in the personality of a place. It can subtly alter one's mood, so it should therefore be handled carefully, but that does not mean timidly. Call upon your own deepest instincts for inspiration."

AGNÈS EMERY, EMERY & CIE

THE COLOR WHEEL WAS FIRST DEVISED BY THE SCIENTIST ISAAC NEWTON, WHO DISCOVERED THAT WHITE LIGHT SPLITS INTO THE COLORS OF THE SPECTRUM WHEN SHONE THROUGH A PRISM. WHEN HE REFRACTED LIGHT THIS WAY, A RAINBOW OF SEVEN COLORS BECAME VISIBLE—RED, ORANGE, YELLOW, GREEN, CYAN (LIGHT BLUE), INDIGO (DARK BLUE), AND VIOLET. IT IS THESE SHADES THAT MAKE UP THE COLOR WHEEL.

White light is really a combination of the three primary colors of red, blue, and yellow. Combinations of these three colors make up the secondary colors of purple, orange, and green. Tertiary colors are those that appear on the wheel between these primary and secondary colors, and are a result of mixing primary and secondary hues together: red-orange, yellow-orange, yellow-green, blue-green, blue-violet and red-violet.

Complementary colors are those that sit opposite one another on the color wheel; blue and orange, red and green, violet and yellow are all complementary. They bring out the vivid tones in each other's hues, creating strong contrasts. Harmonious colors are those that sit next to one another on the wheel and work well together, such as tones of yellow through to terra-cotta, or eggplant to violet.

Using colors according to their natural associations on the color wheel can be a bright and vivid exercise in color combining if you choose the darker shades on the spectrum. But equally, if you use subtler shades of the main colors, and their many associated tones, a more gentle picture emerges that can be just as satisfying.

COLOR AND LIGHT

The texture of paint itself will make a difference to how a color is perceived (see Paints and Finishes, pages 18–19) and this is because of the way it reflects natural light. Matte and chalky paints such as those made by Farrow & Ball and Fine Paints of Europe give depth to a room, thereby making it seem bigger. Shiny, glossy paints and finishes such as silk latex on walls and eggshell on woodwork tend to make a room look smaller, because they reflect the light back rather than absorbing it. This process is the same for both light and dark colors.

The reason why trying to reproduce Rajasthan pink on a bedroom wall in Ireland or a muted Swedish oxblood red in a Mediterranean hacienda will create a paint mistake is also the effect of natural light. To create the desired effect you would have to choose "muddied" tones of a similar color in the northern hemisphere or use the same color ramped up to a vivid tone where the sun shines brightly.

Where natural light is limited, it is actually a good idea to use color. Brilliant white used in the northern hemisphere actually produces an ugly gray effect, especially when artificial light is thrown on it. It is far better to use off-whites mixed with yellow ocher, raw umber, or burnt umber-toned pigments to soften the effect. Francesca Wezel says: "After 20 years of working with colors, the shades that work best in the northern hemisphere are off-whites, fawns, taupes, yellows, and terra-cottas." Even within the northern hemisphere, the natural light is different in Scandinavia than it is in mainland Europe. In the Nordic countries blue works

better when it is mixed with gray tones, altogether more faded than the knocked-back tones of blue mixed with beige that would work in Seattle, New York, or Amsterdam.

GETTING THE WHITE RIGHT

Too often home decorators, faced with an array of off-white tins of paint and color charts, will opt for the shade they have heard of. Magnolia has a lot to answer for. It's not even on the pure spectrum, either in paint terms or in color terms. Its poor reputation these days stems from an overuse of it during the 1980s and 1990s as a poor-quality, vinyl-based contractors' paint that was tinted with a little too many pink tones. It was deemed uncontroversial, a safe bet. Nowadays, thankfully, there are myriad shades of elegant off-white and neutrals that are worth exploring as a base color for rooms.

Paint technology, like everything else in our lives, is changing. A more eco-friendly approach to ingredients and manufacturing processes has resulted in more planet-friendly paint products. Francesca's Paints in London has championed some truly amazing limewash and eco-latex paints. In her Battersea headquarters, Francesca Wezel performs amazing paint alchemy to produce natural paints using limewash, natural pigments, and other eco-friendly raw materials to create stunning colors that are at the couture end of the decorator's toolbox. She is an acknowledged expert in paints and palettes, which range from almost translucent off-white shades of alabaster and white truffle to stronger tones inspired by a sense of place.

ROOM FOR COLOR

OPPOSITE TOP LEFT In Hilton McConnico's Paris house turquoise green and acid yellow combine to make a tart but smart palette, especially when outlined with black detailing on furniture, drapes, and accessories. This is unusual but uplifting.

OPPOSITE TOP RIGHT In Jamie Drake's New York apartment, one of his signature colors, a simply splendid powder pink, provides both decoration and visual interest in a pared-down space.

OPPOSITE BOTTOM LEFT Kitchen designer Johnny Grey is renowned for his sense of color and for mixing materials and shapes. This combination of steel, marble, bubblegum pink, and cornflower blue provides hints of Mexico.

OPPOSITE BOTTOM RIGHT Dark chocolate walls are brought to life with plump yellow pillows and ceramics in a room that is traditional, but with a colorful twist.

ABOVE RIGHT Seaside artifacts and framed textiles set against walls the color of cloudless skies create the perfect nautical palette of red, white, and blue.

IF A WHOLE ROOM CONJURES A COMPLETE PICTURE, THEN THE WALLS SHOULD BE THE BLANK CANVAS STARTING POINT. INSPIRATION MAY TAKE THE FORM OF A KEY PIECE OF FURNITURE OR THE UPHOLSTERY, THE LEVEL OF NATURAL LIGHT, OR AN ARCHITECTURAL FOCAL POINT SUCH AS A FIREPLACE OR A HIGH, ORNATE CEILING.

Color is a personal thing, but it is good to bear in mind the general principles before you start playing with color. Restraint, rather than rampant adventures with pigment, often produces the best results. If you want to create a strong, sure sense of color, many designers advocate avoiding saturated shades on all four walls in favor of well-placed accents around the room. This could take the form of a single wall in a robust shade, or brightly-colored accessories such as drapes, throws, pillows, and lamps used to provide punctuated points of color in the room.

Establishing a mix of tone, texture, and scale in a range of harmonious shades to create a welcoming whole is often the most successful way of creating a cohesive scheme. Using paint on wood paneling, woodwork, and floors is important, too, if you wish to tie together all the elements in a space.

Paint will often look darker when used over a large area of wall, so when choosing paint colors, select paint samples that are a couple of shades lighter than your perceived finished color. Play around with shades and colors before you commit them to walls. It's best to experiment by painting on a test patch of color before buying all your paint, as often the color you have in your head may be different from what is actually in the can.

LOOK AT THE SPACE

Color can be used as a tool to contract or enlarge a space, create a cozy atmosphere, disguise awkward architectural features, and enhance or diminish natural light.

Darker colors such as rich burgundies, stormy blues, and heritage greens will visually bring the walls together and make a room feel smaller and more intimate, while whites and off-whites will create airy surroundings, allowing light to filter onto all surfaces.

Some colors have a natural affinity for certain spaces, such as blues, greens, and whites in bathrooms, where water and mirrors reflect and refract the colors, creating the sense of a seascape indoors. In kitchens where wooden cupboards and surfaces abound, pale neutrals work as good companions to mid-tone woods such as oak and beech, while glossy, sleek contemporary cabinets in black, white, or lacquer red all benefit from white or off-white walls, so the units can do the color-talking.

PAINTED FLOORS

Painted floors are so very á la mode and a great way of completing a palette in a room, both anchoring a scheme and providing a rich surface underfoot for colors to work with. For a sleek finish it's best to use gloss or eggshell paint, which provides a pleasing patina and is tough and durable for foot traffic. To create a vintage look, dilute the paint with mineral spirits. Brush on the paint, then remove the top layer with muslin to distress the surface.

"If I am feeling neutral it is linen white, as it goes with everything. But it depends, as every room is different: it depends on the architecture, the light coming in though the window, what way the windows face, and if there are any obstructions outside. All these make a difference." KIT KEMP, HOTEL DESIGNER

PAINTS AND FINISHES

COLOR WILL PERFORM IN DIFFERENT WAYS ACCORDING TO HOW IT IS APPLIED TO WALLS AND FLOORS. MATTE SURFACES GIVE DEPTH TO A ROOM AND MAKE IT APPEAR LARGER, WHILE GLOSS SURFACES REFLECT LIGHT RATHER THAN ABSORB IT. IN DARK SPACES IT IS BEST TO USE SOME FORM OF COLOR RATHER THAN BRILLIANT WHITE OR GRAY, WHICH WILL EMPHASIZE LACK OF LIGHT.

When thinking about which type of paint to use, consider the size of your room, the amount of natural light it receives, and whether you want the atmosphere to be one of relaxation or activity, and the use formal or informal.

Matte Latex paint is water-based, easy to apply, and quick to dry. It normally has a low VOC (volatile organic compound) rating, which means it is kinder to the environment than harsh gloss paints. While it is wipeable it may not be washable. It can be diluted with water to lighten its shade, and is suitable for interior plaster walls, lining wallpaper used to cover imperfect walls, and ceilings.

Vinyl Silk or Satin Latex is tougher and more durable than matte latex and has a mid-sheen finish. It is washable and very suitable for walls that experience high traffic, such as halls, stairways, and landings.

Gloss is an oil-based paint that is tough, shiny, and less environmentally friendly than latex paint. Its ultra sheen finish works well on woodwork, furniture, and floors, as well as metal. It is sometimes used for walls and ceilings, too, in more daring schemes. Apply a primer undercoat first.

Eggshell is the oil-based equivalent of vinyl satin and gives a mid-range sheen for woodwork. It is also known as satinwood or semi-gloss and doesn't need an undercoat.

FAR LEFT Amazing finishes can be achieved by treating fresh plaster in a certain way. Here Linda Barker overlaid a thin layer of plaster with a second one, applied with a bevel-edged trowel to produce a slightly mottled effect. An application of wax over the top provides a pleasing translucent finish.

LEFT Both glorious and glamorous, this symphony of surfaces was composed by Solis Betancourt from a pleasing juxtaposition of elegant period furniture, a mirrored table, and a glossy Provence blue screen whose sheen dances with light.

ABOVE In a space designed by Linda Barker, the wall and its colors provide the decoration while everything else in the room is very understated. Blocks of color in slate, elephant gray, and dove allow contemporary chairs to appear to meld into the wall.

Water-based Eggshell is a more environmentally friendly version of eggshell, with a low sheen and low VOC rating.

Limewash is a traditional paint finish that allows a wall to breathe. It is particularly suitable for bare plaster walls, cement render, or skimmed, unfilled walls where some natural moisture is present, such as stone farmhouses. It is not suitable for use on wood, or any non-porous surface, but can be used on top of lining paper if it is applied over a base coat of matte latex. Always apply it using a brush rather than a roller. Available in interior and exterior versions, it produces an opaque, textured velvety look.

Eco Latex is a new type of zero VOC-content paint with an ultra matte finish and low odor that is gaining popularity. Several paint producers are creating an ever-widening range of palettes, including Auro Organics, Nutshell Natural Paints, Ecolibrium, and Eco Chic by Oliver Heath. It's suitable for use on walls.

Floor Paint is a low VOC-rated paint with an eggshell finish suitable for wooden and concrete floors, produced by Farrow & Ball and Benjamin Moore, among others.

Varnishes are available in a variety of finishes, from dead flat to eggshell. Normally they have low VOC ratings and are used for protecting surfaces covered with water-based paint, whether for walls or for wood surfaces. Even varnishing very flat finishes will subtly alter the opacity of

the surface so bear this mind when you are settling on a finish and final color for your walls, and test out a small area before you commit.

Wood Stain can be natural or colored and is used on surfaces such as floors and furniture. It's best used on areas of low traffic as it doesn't wear as well as paint.

Kitchen and Bathroom Paint is devised especially for use in kitchens, bathrooms, and basements. More moisture and mildew resistant than conventional paints, it is washable and available in satin or gloss finishes.

Metallic Paints often look like gold leaf but are also available in silver, copper, and bronze as well as gold forms for applying to metal on top of an undercoat. New metallic wall paints have also been developed to provide a glamorous shimmer for living rooms and dining rooms. Sherwin Williams produce a metallic-finish paint.

Glitter Paint is a topcoat glazed paint that dries clear and leaves a glint of glitter over any matte latex.

Buttermilk Paints are specialty traditional paints once used to dull the glossy surfaces of oil paintings, but are best known as the type of paint the Shakers used for their decorative painted woodwork. The non-reflective flat finish is prone to marking, but their natural ingredients make them a good choice for allergy sufferers.

sunshine
& citrus

primrose
pampas
straw
hay bale
corn
honey
cheetah
stoneground
gilt
cornfield
barleytwist
desert sand
maize
soft clay
wheaten
parmigiana
maple syrup
citrus zest
summer sunshine
canary yellow
citron
butternut squash
monet yellow
cadmium yellow
provence
lemon drop
cape sunshine
toscana
tangerine
tangiers
gold
mango
pumpkin
marigold

ALL ABOUT YELLOW

Yellow is the color of sunshine, upbeat and uplifting, not shy about shouting its presence. But every can of yellow paint should also perhaps come with a Caution: Handle with Care warning as it can be a tricky color to get right.

Choosing a perfect yellow is not easy because its tone intensifies when painted on walls, more so than many other colors. While you may be seduced by the sunny shades on a tiny paint chip, the overall effect of even a single wall, or indeed a whole room of the same color, can be overwhelming in reality.

The difficult child of the paint world, yellow is often unpredictable and can be quite contrary in a light-filled room. The glorious bright tones we associate with summer sun are often delicate to translate to northern hemisphere walls, such as New York apartments or an English town house, where light may not be in such abundant and regular supply.

As a general rule yellow is most at home in the natural light of the southern hemisphere, from Mexico to the Mediterranean and across to Africa and Australasia. This bright light has a more favorable effect on strong yellow than does cold northern light. In the north, it's best to knock off any acid edges with warmer tones of soft gold or pale ocher, which are more sophisticated. Surface finish is important too. If a paint is very matte it will absorb more light and therefore make a space look larger.

David Oliver of The Paint Library in London says, "Trying to translate the color of Provençal sunflower fields to your kitchen walls can sometimes land you with a bad omelet shade, which is certainly not life enhancing. The answer is to experiment by painting a wooden box with a pale neutral undercoat, then applying coats of your chosen color. It is important with strong shades to gain an impression of how they will bathe an entire room with the color, and how they will change throughout the day according to light levels."

Yellow is associated with sunny, uplifting emotions. But the precise shade of yellow that you carry in your mind's eye does not always translate to the paint can or prepared wall—this is true of yellow more than any other color—which is why your chosen color can sometimes disappoint on the wall. To work in bright tones yellow ideally needs warm, sunny natural light to bring out its real color values. The stronger tones are often best used as accents, such as ceramics, lighting, or pillows, or in small areas within a room, say one wall or an alcove.

Across the Sunshine & Citrus palette yellow with a hint of black veers towards a muddy green, while red tones provide a warmth that will make it suitable for teaming with earthy rust colors and a wide variety of natural woods, from pale beech to deep mahogany.

Yellow's reputation as a fresh and lively sunny color means it is often used in kitchens, where a sunny outlook, an atmosphere of bustling activity, and a sense of purpose will be enhanced by this palette. It is said to stimulate the brain, promote a sense of open-mindedness, and also aid concentration, so it works well in pantries, utility rooms, and home offices, where transient activities or bursts of concentrated work take place.

Relaxing spaces such as living rooms, bedrooms, and bathrooms do not usually gain much in ambiance or restful atmosphere from being bathed in yellow, although paler shades may work nicely and become especially inviting when used in harmonizing or contrasting tones. Francesca Wezel of Francesca's Paints cites soft ocher yellow as one of her bestselling paint colors, alongside off-whites, fawns, taupe and terra-cotta.

Strong citric shades are best used in rooms suffused with generous amounts of warm natural light like that of the southern hemisphere.

PROVENCE

"I have been using yellow more
recently, in different ways and
only in small and medium-scale
rooms. When I want to surprise
or provoke an emotional reaction
I use yellow because it affects
your mood, transfers energy,
and promotes joy and happiness."

ILARIA MIANI

KEY LIME

MAIZE

GOLD

SAFFRON

USING YELLOW Yellow can be difficult to work with, but it is rewarding when you get it right. While acid yellows can be cold unless they have red or brown elements in them, lemon yellow can create a warm and inviting palette, especially at the softer buttery yellow and ocher range in the spectrum. These are often the most successful shades to work with. Too often when trying to create a crisp citric tone it is easy to end up with a sickly acidic shade that calls for sunglasses rather than admiring glances, so exercise caution and restraint when working within this range.

Remember that any one color, and especially yellow, can look completely different depending on the level of natural and artificial lighting in a space. If possible, paint large pieces of lining paper in your chosen color and attach them temporarily to the walls you intend to paint. Check on them throughout the day and notice how they change color according to the light levels. This is a particularly useful exercise if you are planning to paint an entire room in the same color. Once you gain an impression of the true intensity of the color at the times of day when you are likely to be using the room, you might decide to paint just one wall in the color, or indeed to choose a different color entirely.

Colorwashing, the technique of using several layers of watered-down paint, works very well for yellow as it is a color that calls for subtlety, especially in a period house, where strong shades are best used as broken color or as accents. If you are deliberately seeking to use uniform, bright tones then these are best suited to contemporary settings.

Yellow's complementary shade on the color wheel is blue. While rich, deep yellow and blue are a classic and traditional palette for country kitchens, these two complementaries often work

Novices in yellow should stick to the softer ends of the sunshine spectrum for the best results.

best in subtle, muted combinations, with the yellow pushed towards a pale sand-like palette and the blue shifted to a muted blue-gray, almost Scandinavian in influence. Francesca Wezel of Francesca's Paints believes that blue and yellow together can look wrong if combined with one another in tones that are too strong. They also tend to look quite old fashioned.

Yellow also works well with greens and oranges, providing crisp uplifting palettes that are quite bold to the eye. Experiment with tangerine tones and pale primrose, or sunny yellows and deep leaf greens. This is not really a color for using often on doors or woodwork in the strong tones, although sandy ocher colors or faded primrose can work if teamed with pale gray walls and a splash of yellow on a fireplace mantel which could make a pleasing Scandinavian-style palette.

As an accent color, strong imperial yellow works very well, but is most successful in rooms that benefit from plenty of strong light. You can get away much more easily with sherbet shades or jewel-bright tones by using them on small areas or as zingy punctuation points throughout a room on pillows, curtains, or rugs.

For accenting yellow rooms, I particularly favor steely gray or black to provide both smart contrast and graphic definition for the space— this can be quite crisp but a sure statement. Use these defining tones to contain and enhance yellow on pillow piping; architectural elements such as baseboards, doors, and dados; on lamps and lampshades; or furniture detailing.

OPPOSITE TOP LEFT Subtle tones of pale yellow ocher tinged with green make a sharp complement to mauve-blue details on furniture and in paintings. The palette is grounded with a smart slate gray floor.

OPPOSITE TOP RIGHT In this Los Angeles home a bitter lemon scheme has been applied to bookshelves and a wall, providing a vivid counterpoint to a big collection of art books, perhaps to stimulate an enquiring mind .

OPPOSITE BOTTOM LEFT In urban England a buttercup yellow can only thrive in this kitchen/dining space due to massive amounts of natural light and an interesting monochrome pillar placed directly alongside the building.

OPPOSITE BOTTOM RIGHT In a hunting lodge in the Périgord region of France, rough plastered walls are colorwashed in pale tones of layered ocher and yellow for a timeless feel.

sunshine & citrus | lemon

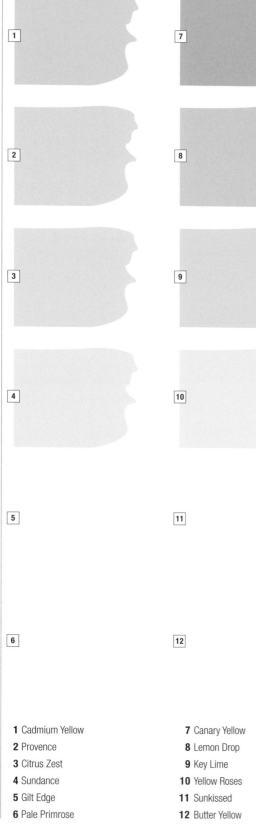

ABOVE Ilaria Miani's Italian farmhouse kitchen combines clean lemon tones with a limed oak-raftered ceiling and a stonework floor. Black detailing in the form of lampshades, suspended shelving, and painted stripes on the table brings a smart finish and a slight contemporary twist to the space.

Yellows range from delicate primrose and enriching ocher shades to acid, uncompromising cadmium yellow. Experiment with muted tones to begin with as pure yellow can sometimes jar the senses.

1 Cadmium Yellow
2 Provence
3 Citrus Zest
4 Sundance
5 Gilt Edge
6 Pale Primrose

7 Canary Yellow
8 Lemon Drop
9 Key Lime
10 Yellow Roses
11 Sunkissed
12 Butter Yellow

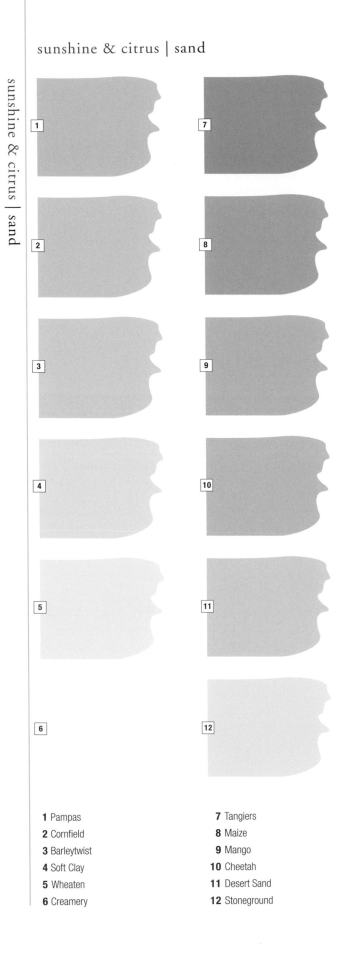

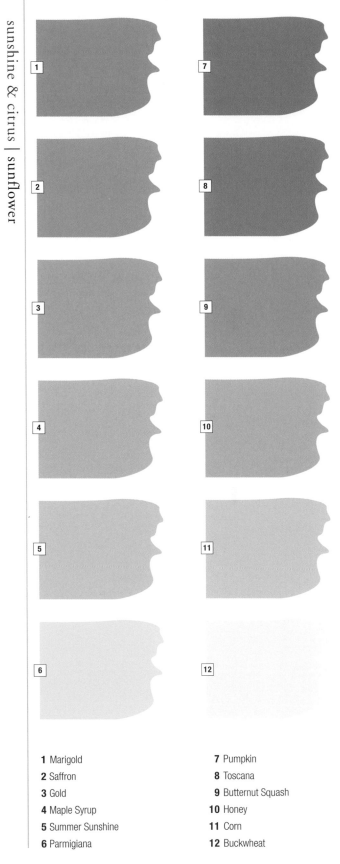

1 Pampas	**7** Tangiers
2 Cornfield	**8** Maize
3 Barleytwist	**9** Mango
4 Soft Clay	**10** Cheetah
5 Wheaten	**11** Desert Sand
6 Creamery	**12** Stoneground

1 Marigold	**7** Pumpkin
2 Saffron	**8** Toscana
3 Gold	**9** Butternut Squash
4 Maple Syrup	**10** Honey
5 Summer Sunshine	**11** Corn
6 Parmigiana	**12** Buckwheat

"For each definite shade of yellow I would choose different references and matching colors that are sympathetic with them. Complementary tones for yellow in a traditional setting with antique, aged, or mahogany furniture are shades of chestnut or maroon brown." ILARIA MIANI

THIS PAGE A kitchen decorated in classic lemon and cornflower blue, which takes its cue from Cornishware china, demonstrates the easy comfort of a successful complementary palette—both colors bring out the best in one another.

OPPOSITE Strong lemon combined with complementary shades of milky gray-green and burgundy red makes for a rich and reassuring atmosphere in a rustic French retreat.

lemon

The lemon palette ranges from brilliant tones of sharp citrus at the vivid end of the spectrum to soft, understated pale primrose at the other. Citrus lemon is a crisp, lively color that works particularly well in kitchens, where it is uplifting, friendly, and outgoing. As a color it is known to stimulate the mind, encouraging people to be alert, activating their memory, and encouraging communication, so it is also a good choice for home offices or studies. For the same reasons it is less restful in a living room, although paler shades can certainly work well in relaxing spaces. Team lemon with crisp bright white, dark oaky brown, or jet black for a sharp color focus.

Use very bright lemon, such as cadmium yellow or acid lemon-green, only as accents in a room or on very small areas at a time; lemon is on the warm spectrum, yet can often jolt the senses if it becomes too bright. Yellows with too much green will veer towards unflattering limey shades, especially under artificial light, so steer away from such palettes if you are after a sharp lemon shade.

Traditional French Provençal houses often feature lemons of all tones as a signature color, while imperial yellow was often seen in the smart Georgian houses of 19th-century London. Nowadays you are most likely to see lemon used in contemporary urban settings, often as statement walls in midtown lofts, or as accent pieces of furniture, such as chairs, in modern workplaces.

country retreat

A Provençal bedroom is pale, interesting, and restful thanks to primrose walls and complementary powder blue bedding. Natural stonework, buttermilk-painted wood, and a bleached brown floor tie the scheme together.

green accent

Warm but muted, hazy walls have been achieved by layering colorwashes one on another. An earth-toned floor and an elegant mahogany table work as counterpoints, allowing contrasting lapis green ceramics to take center stage.

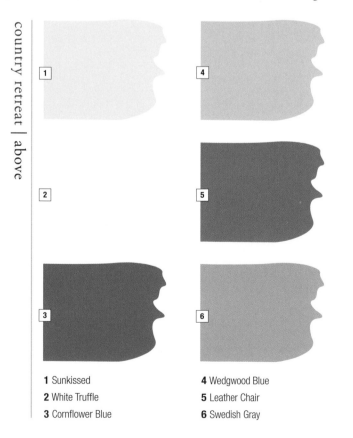

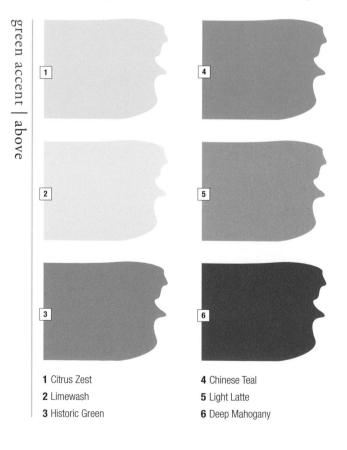

country retreat | above

1   4

2   5

3   6

1 Sunkissed   **4** Wedgwood Blue

2 White Truffle   **5** Leather Chair

3 Cornflower Blue   **6** Swedish Gray

green accent | above

1   4

2   5

3   6

1 Citrus Zest   **4** Chinese Teal

2 Limewash   **5** Light Latte

3 Historic Green   **6** Deep Mahogany

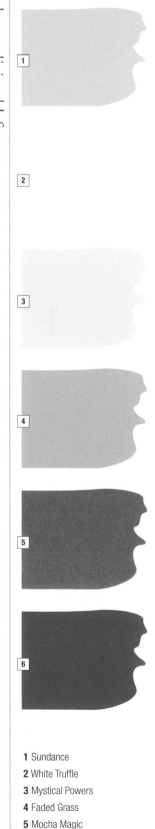

breezy living
A rich honey yellow infused with reddish tones is perfectly combined with rust-red notes on the shades and in the soft furnishings. Neutral flooring fades into the background to allow the reddish browns of a carved Indian closet and a rattan coffee table to create a relaxed, welcoming atmosphere.

1 Sundance
2 White Truffle
3 Mystical Powers
4 Faded Grass
5 Mocha Magic
6 Red Brick Wall

"The first color I ever made into a paint, called Christophe's White, is the one that still sells the most. It combines three basic pigments, raw umber, burnt umber, and yellow ocher— all warm shades. It is perfect for northern climes, as it takes away the grayness present in the natural light and warms up a space, without resorting to the dreaded 'magnolia.'"

FRANCESCA WEZEL, FRANCESCA'S PAINTS

sand

Heading towards the soft yellow end of the spectrum, sandy colors include pale ocher tones where the yellow is dulled by a hint of brown as well as deeper wheat, stone, and desert shades. These sandy shades are much more approachable and certainly more peaceful than lemon tones and are popular colors to work with, often forming the basis of an interesting neutral palette. They work well as part of an earthy palette, too, coupled with deep terracottas or warm cinnamon. And they can stand alone, providing calm, neutral backdrops on which you can layer accent colors from other palettes. For accent colors, add sunflower accessories in the form of tablecloths, artwork, or soft furnishings to sandy-colored walls and furniture and you will impart a sense of "sunshine by osmosis." Or use harmonious tones of sandstone, beige, or taupe for a multi-layered look that brings in other off-white or neutral tones.

Layers of texture also work well in sandy palettes, hinting at the desert and the seashore. Add this in the form of fabrics, rough ceramics, or pottery, or even on the walls, by using rough plasterwork or applying specialist glazes or a colorwash, which give the flavor of a faded fresco wall. At the deeper end of the spectrum, butternut squash and popcorn yellows with more of an orange bias are warming. Team them with browns and subtle taupes for a cohesive scheme that works as well in the northern U.S. as it does in warmer countries.

THIS PAGE A totally natural palette of pale sand and stone is a masterclass in using colors that are close to one another in a single palette, known as harmonious or analogous colors.

OPPOSITE Sandy ocher walls provide a pale but inviting backdrop for fabrics and upholstery in rich earthy shades.

cool provence

Simple French country architecture benefits from sand-colored walls that enhance and define yellow-tinged, textured stonework. The space is elegant, with earthy accents in the flagstone floor and off-white furniture. Woodwork and accessories in a muted blue-gray echo the lavender-washed landscape.

cool provence | opposite

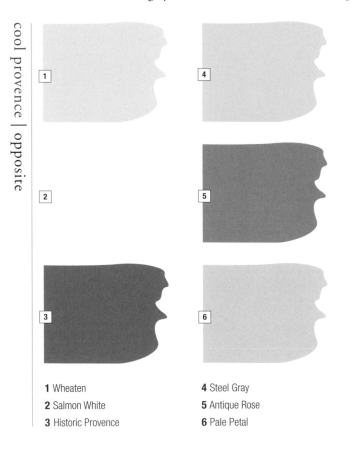

1 Wheaten   **4** Steel Gray

2 Salmon White   **5** Antique Rose

3 Historic Provence   **6** Pale Petal

Perfect sand shades are those that include delicate traces of yellow, red, or brown. Barely noticeable, these small tints provide a natural warmth, especially on unpapered plaster walls.

field of sand

This Pennsylvanian dining room takes its keynote tones of pale and deep yellows, complementary reds and greens, and shades of orange from a folk art wall hanging. Rich sandy notes combine with apple red and deep green for a bold combination set against pale walls and an ocher-toned painted floor.

field of sand | above

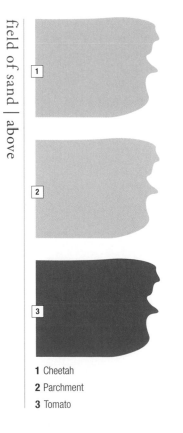
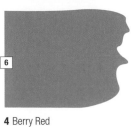

1 Cheetah   **4** Berry Red

2 Parchment   **5** Naranja

3 Tomato   **6** Bowling Green

"Rooms that use color lavishly are intriguing, intoxicating, and inviting. The selection of a palette that you love is a sure-fire way to bring your personality home. Whether you opt for a multitude of vibrant accents to spark a more sedate surround, or you go for full-throttle color everywhere, the introduction of color guarantees a smashing interior." JAMIE DRAKE

THIS PAGE Rich golden tones applied as broken color in a living room chime perfectly with a gilded fireplace, deep olive green woodwork, and subtle tones—earthy brown on the furniture and deep reds on the carpet.

OPPOSITE Mexican architect Manolo Mestre has layered deep sunflower shades onto rough plaster in this light-filled home in Careyes on the Pacific Coast. Raw tones of burnt sienna and squab pillows in fuchsia bring further surprise and delight to this scheme.

sunflower

The enriching tones of sunflower fields and the vivid ocher shades associated with Mexican haciendas are colors that are also capable of working in northern climates. They are at the warmer end of the sunshine spectrum, with a yellow basis that includes enough orange in its make-up to survive under a cooler light and not give off too greenish a glow. These strong shades also work well as accent colors against leaf greens, opulent blues, and deep reds—palettes in which deep base colors call for sharp counterpoints.

New York-based Jamie Drake is one of a few designers who embraces bright color. He possesses an innate skill for infusing rooms with vivid tones that simply sing in a space, providing instant uplift and a vibrant atmosphere. He often combines such colors with bold and eclectic pieces of furniture to really bring a room to life.

Elsewhere, in Mexico, architect Alex Possenbacher uses rich burnt umber-tinged shades of sunflower and deep corn that bring pueblo style to life. These colors are perfectly at home in the sun-filled setting of the Pacific Coast, where their roasting tones animate the coolest, darkest part of a house. With their warming burnt sienna quality, they also work in spaces where there is a cooler, grayer light. Good for cooking and dining spaces, sunflower shades also work well in outdoor rooms, verandas or patios, where they bring instant sunshine to seating and food preparation areas.

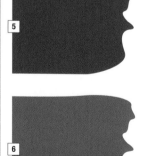

1 Summer Sunshine
2 Butternut Squash
3 Beige Sand
4 Venetian Sunset
5 Bright Fuchsia
6 Earthworks

sunshine spectrum Jamie

Drake's innate sense of color simply sings in this warming bedroom with its perfect saturated yellow walls and toning drapes. A yellow bed throw and upholstered chairs tie the scheme together, while an eclectic mix of wooden furniture creates a pleasing earth base for this rich palette.

chic adobe
Mexican architect Alex Possenbacher often uses indigenous colors such as rich yellow ocher on textured plaster surfaces to create layers of warm broken color. Used on three-quarter walls in this vaulted bedroom, the strong tones are inviting rather than over-indulgent as they command attention without dominating the space.

1 Marigold
2 Brown Sugar
3 Pumice
4 New White
5 Texas Rose
6 Mississippi Mud

cranberry & orange

plaster pink
venetian rose
baby pink
strawberry milkshake
ladybug
cherry blossom
rose garden
pink lipstick
cotton candy
flame
coral
shrimp
tuscan red
nectarine
tangerine dream
carrot stick
russet
brick pink
nasturtium
raspberry mousse
venetian red
mulberry
poppy
cherry
jaipur
pomegranate
sun-dried tomato
crimson
racing red
redcurrant
rich burgundy
chili pepper
cadmium
moroccan red

ALL ABOUT RED

Red is powerful and evocative, sensual and symbolic, a primary color that is confident and always ready to take a stand. Hot, fiery, and passionate, it is an established favorite with designers, proving its versatility for adding space-enhancing comfort, conveying a bold design vision, and providing life-affirming jolts of color as accents.

In color preference tests red is always more popular than yellow, green, or orange. It has negative connotations too, though. Think about fire, flame, and danger, or the color of anarchy and revolution. On the one hand, beware of its power, and on the other, seize the moment and be brave with some purposeful shades. Interestingly, women often cite red as their favorite color, whereas men are more likely to choose blue.

Red is an historical primary color. Red paint, formed originally from naturally occurring red-oxide, was as popular in Pompeii as it was in Native American buildings. American barn red is a deep earthy red that endures today, as do the rich russet tones found in Swedish interiors on painted furniture and on vernacular buildings, often teamed with white woodwork.

You cannot help but react to rooms decorated with vibrant red. People who choose to decorate with this color are often strong characters, with a zest for life and a need for excitement. Bold red shades will bathe a room with constant warmth, even one that does not receive much natural light, as well as increase adrenalin levels slightly on a first encounter.

Rich reds, the colors of red wine and roses, hearts and flowers, also promote energy, instill a sense of protection and offer a feeling of reassurance. All the assets of the red

From raspberry to rose and tomato to tangerine, the red palette is fiery and fierce, courageous and passionate.

carpet rolled into one if you will. And as a night-time color, red is second to none, producing an enveloping reflective warmth. Many neutral colors are natural partners for reds, from pale biscuit and wheat, to grays of varying intensity, from silver to slate. Even black brings out the vibrancy of red—it is a classic combination in Japanese interiors.

The drama queen of the color palette, red is always dressed to impress.

From the softer shades of rose and baby pink, via coral and flame to the big bold ruby reds, the red palette works in small spaces as a saturated shade on all surfaces just as well as it does on a single wall, or as an accent color in a larger space. It really comes into its own in analogous palettes though, where shades of red, rose, and flame fall together in a loud statement or a subtle conglomeration, depending on the final mix of shades (think of Campari and soda, the embers of a real fire, the ruby red shades of tomatoes or pomegranates). The reds of nature—colors of a sunset, soft fruits, and poison berries, bright poppies and ladybugs—are all able to mingle successfully in a room just as much as they do in nature.

In decoration, red traditionally often signified luxury, particularly when partnered with gilt or gold textures such as fringing or opulent picture frames. As red pigment was expensive until synthetic substitutes were discovered in the mid-19th century, its presence in state rooms, picture galleries, and grand dining rooms was intended as a statement of wealth and exclusivity.

Calming the natural electricity of red is best done with pale neutrals. Clean white lends an instant Swedish feel, while buttery creams lend rustic charm, and textured jutes and linens give a fresh contemporary country edge. If you want to increase the color temperature even more though, add in a fresh zingy lime, in the form of temporary accessories such as a vase of *Alchemilla mollis* or a white dish of limes to create instant impact.

ROSE GARDEN

COTTON CANDY

TUSCAN PINK

NECTARINE

MOROCCAN RED

MULBERRY

"When choosing colors, think about the colors you like to wear. Mixing colors is a form of expression and, if you like, a form of language, like the way one dresses." DAVID OLIVER, THE PAINT LIBRARY

USING RED Red is a versatile color, looking crisp, contemporary, and smart one minute when combined with textured slate gray upholstery, or simple and rustic when used in tomato shades as a strong accent color on woodwork and furniture in an off-white room.

Red is a good analogous palette, working in partnership with crimson as it becomes deep plum or purple or before it merges into the green-blue and gray-blue. At the paler end of the spectrum, rozy tones ranging from muddy 1950s muted shades to more vibrant cotton candy and rouge pink are perfect for feminine bedrooms and summery living rooms or kitchens, where sugar plum shades work well in combination with mint or leaf green, pale woods, deeper truer reds, or a lilac palette. Introduce reds into a room in the form of luscious velvet drapes or vibrant pillows if you do not feel bold enough to make such a positive and dramatic color statement by drenching your walls in saturated red tones.

David Oliver of the Paint Library feels strongly that one of the most common mistakes made when using deeper shades or strong color on the walls is to paint the baseboard, cornice, and molding in too pale a shade. The effect to avoid is the sense of "picture framing" or accentuating the perimeters or boundaries of a room with white woodwork. White surfaces are more visible to the naked eye than dark surfaces, which absorb light. As a guide try to keep the baseboard a shade not more than 50 percent darker or lighter than the wall and floor colors, so that the contrast is not too emphatic.

Red looks wonderful when partnered with any of the neutral colors, such as pale oaten beiges and grays to chocolate browns and deepest slate black.

Painting your woodwork in shades of red, when paired with walls in a compatible depth of color, is a definite design statement.

Dining areas are often a good room in which to indulge a passion for deep red. The color is known to create a rush of adrenalin, bringing with it a heightened enjoyment of food and convivial conversation. North-facing rooms are positively warmed by red tones, especially in winter months.

Hotel designer Kit Kemp tends to use strong colors such as deep mulberry on walls that don't receive any light, such as basements and dark corners. "I actually use contrasting strong colors on different walls to jolt the eye—we have done this with The Soho Hotel. This makes people forget that there is no actual daylight in the space and also pulls your eyes round the corners. I also put a strong color at the end of a corridor to pull your eye to what could be a very boring space."

Bedrooms may not be the most ambient spaces for deep reds, as rest and relaxation may be hard to come by in such a stimulating environment. But dining rooms, living rooms and kitchens—which enjoy more activity—are all rooms that red likes. And hallways bathed in red will say a lot about you.

OPPOSITE TOP LEFT Layers of broken color in shades of plaster pink and pale orange evoke the rough-textured walls of Tuscan farmhouses in Rupert Spira's London home.

OPPOSITE TOP RIGHT Shocking pink furniture accents provoke a strong harmony with vivid flame ceiling detailing in a contemporary apartment designed by Karim Rashid.

OPPOSITE BOTTOM Red and orange combine with one another surprisingly well, especially as accent colors in this cool, neutral space in Mexico, designed by Jenny Armit, that enjoys plenty of natural light.

With all the assets and symbols of the red carpet rolled into one, vigorous and assertive red calls for courage—wherever it is used, it makes its presence felt, so be prepared for it to dominate a room.

cranberry & orange | rose

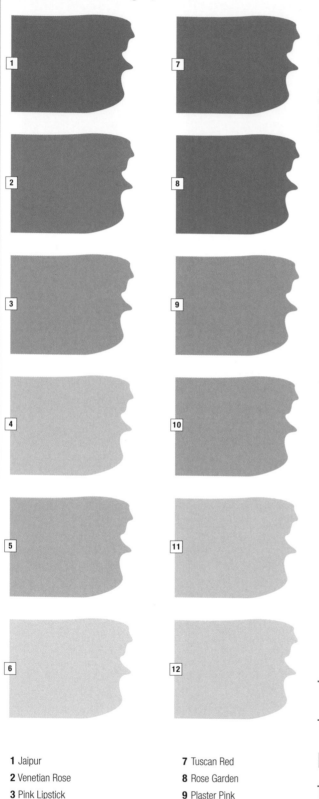

1 Jaipur
2 Venetian Rose
3 Pink Lipstick
4 Pink Dream
5 Cotton Candy
6 Sugar Almond

7 Tuscan Red
8 Rose Garden
9 Plaster Pink
10 Brick Pink
11 Strawberry Milkshake
12 Baby Pink

The red range encompasses feminine, but not too sugary, rose pinks, hot flames in the form of rich oranges, and, at the racy end of the spectrum, hot luscious reds that make their presence felt.

ABOVE Dusky rose pink tones on walls are cool tones that absorb light. They work equally well in rooms where there is plenty of natural light and in spaces where a color lift is required.

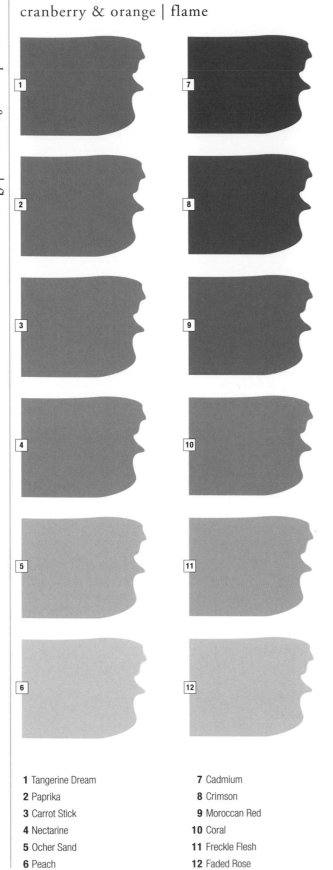

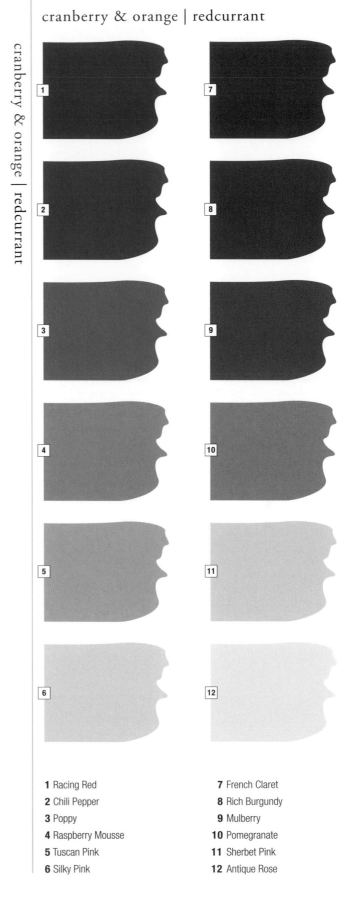

1 Tangerine Dream
2 Paprika
3 Carrot Stick
4 Nectarine
5 Ocher Sand
6 Peach

7 Cadmium
8 Crimson
9 Moroccan Red
10 Coral
11 Freckle Flesh
12 Faded Rose

1 Racing Red
2 Chili Pepper
3 Poppy
4 Raspberry Mousse
5 Tuscan Pink
6 Silky Pink

7 French Claret
8 Rich Burgundy
9 Mulberry
10 Pomegranate
11 Sherbet Pink
12 Antique Rose

"Farrow & Ball Cinder Rose No. 246 is an unusual, fresh mauve-pink color, which works wonderfully as a color to pictures and strong textiles—it is reminiscent of country house bedroom interiors. It has the attractive feeling of over-blown roses in a garden in late summer: a really charming boudoir color, sumptuous and opulent when contrasted with deep purples." SARAH COLE, DIRECTOR, FARROW & BALL

rose

As delicate as a tea rose or as strong as a fuchsia, rose tones are popular, not just for feminine bedrooms but also for breezy kitchens and airy living spaces. The red content in even the palest of baby pinks always provides a warm cast and an inviting ambiance. Dusky muted tones work well in spaces that are used for contemplation, such as studies, libraries, or quiet reading corners in a living room. Partner them with woodwork painted in sophisticated clotted cream shades or create a layered palette by using lavender blues or dusky gray mink in an analogous formation. Astonishingly popular as a color for girls' bedrooms in recent years, rose has escaped the nursery and is now just as likely to be seen making a statement in kitchens, dining rooms, and even bathrooms. Rose is also capable of being smart and sleek when accompanied by complementary shades of rich lime, forest green, or mint, the colors for bringing out the best in the rose spectrum.

But if what you are aiming for is a delicate backdrop, then use analogous tones of soft peach and translucent coral and pair them with a pale steely gray or light tones of barely-there mint for a sophisticated contrast. The paints of Farrow & Ball and Fine Paints of Europe include painterly pale pinks that are perfect for this effect. Rose is a color that is most successful when used in a matte chalky form rather than as a glossy surface, which can make it appear too sickly, detracting from its natural grace.

THIS PAGE Faded tea-rose pink on walls, woodwork, and furniture creates a delicate space in which a light teal green quilt evokes a 1930s color palette. Feminine and inviting, this rustic bedroom is perfectly pink.

OPPOSITE Sugar plum paint on the walls creates a striking "pink punch" background for fuchsia-toned fabrics and harmonious orange bedding. Reds, pinks, and oranges always work surprising well together.

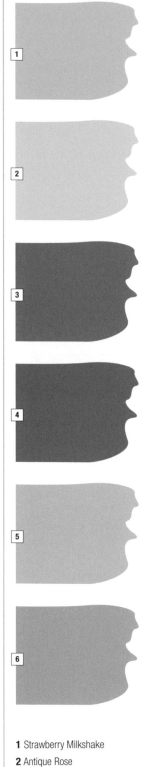

1 Strawberry Milkshake
2 Antique Rose
3 Military Uniform
4 Purple Heart
5 Lilac Gray
6 Gustavian

two-tone rose This exquisite period home
in the Canary Islands draws the clear light of the Atlantic Ocean into and
around its high-ceilinged rooms. A glorious mix of tone-on-tone roses,
faded lilacs, and red-toned bleached boards makes for a wistful, pleasing
palette that changes throughout the day as light travels around the space.

la vie en rose
The Parisian home of designer Agnès Comar employs the garden colors of traditional rose and green leaf to punctuate a muted gray space. Slate gray voile both frames the room and allows diffused light to settle on the jewel-like chairs. The palette takes a red/green complementary story to a pleasing, sophisticated level.

1 Venetian Rose
2 Mimosa
3 Gustavian Gray
4 Evening Dove
5 Kiwi
6 Lavender Blue

"Use signal colors like orange and cranberry to accentuate architectural detail. The use of contrasting colors is especially effective when they are used to highlight features such as arches, entrances, soffits, nooks, and trim. This is an opportunity to play not just with color, but with dimensionality—have fun!" CARL MINCHEW, DIRECTOR OF COLOR TECHNOLOGY, BENJAMIN MOORE

flame

THIS PAGE In John Pardey's Berkshire home he has painted one wall of a narrow corridor a vivid orange in direct contrast to its complementary color, sea blue. Glimpsing the blue wall in the distance with an orange, warming atmosphere as you approach distracts attention away from the narrowness of the space.

OPPOSITE In a French chateau, copper saucepans in rich, reflective tones look as though they were chosen to be displayed for the sole purpose of blending beautifully with the warm apricot colorwashed walls. The melodious mellow palette is perfectly accompanied by a scrubbed refectory table.

Hot, fiery, and uncompromising, the orange story encompasses the vivid shades of tangerine, veering at one end of the spectrum dangerously close to overpowering pillar box reds and at the other to softer Tuscan tones. As with pink, vibrant orange shades can veer towards the tacky and unpleasant, so use them with care. Choose tones that contain a strong amount of brown in them for more of an earthy feel. For a vivid approach, use flame tones with a strong yellow element. Such strong shades never fail to enliven a space, but are not for those whose forays into color amount to a few muted neutrals. The flame palette packs a punch: just think of the number of corporate companies who use orange in their brand identities to grab your attention, or the way "safety" orange is used on the jackets of construction workers. It is therefore best to avoid using strong orange in rooms or places where you wish to create an aura of calm and relaxation.

Rich orange often looks best in tiny spaces such as guest cloakrooms. For a statement, allow a deep tangerine to make a grand appearance on one wall of a contemporary space. Architects of minimalist-style homes often use orange as a decorative element to break up and embolden Brutalist linear rooms. As a warming tone, the deeper shades of russet and amber can make great companions for any style of living space. Think of sun-kissed Italian villas, Provençal farmhouses, and southwestern haciendas.

flame heaven

Striking flame is best saved for small surfaces and accessories. Here, upholstery, a rug, and a painting that includes orange square motifs are the starting point for an entire palette. With such strong accents, the walls must stay neutral so the furniture can do the color talking.

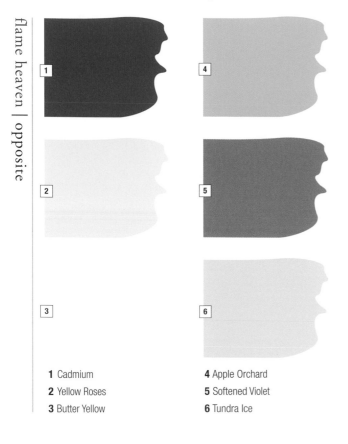

1 Cadmium

2 Yellow Roses

3 Butter Yellow

4 Apple Orchard

5 Softened Violet

6 Tundra Ice

Fiery, passionate shades of orange are extremely good accent colors. Avoid bathing a whole room in these vibrant tones as they are most powerful when used in only part of a room.

tangerine dream

Burnt flame dado-height panels of color anchor a scheme that comprises deep terra-cotta and cream checkerboard tiling and multi-colored panes at the window. The result is warm, earthy, and enriching, combining a pale but rich mascarpone shade on the walls and bedding with the rich rust.

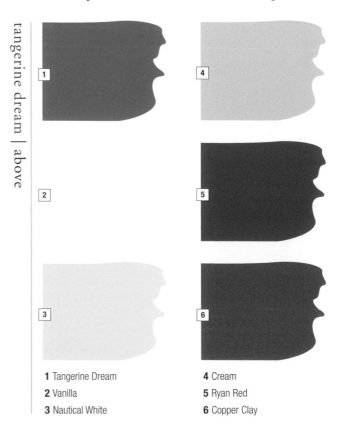

1 Tangerine Dream

2 Vanilla

3 Nautical White

4 Cream

5 Ryan Red

6 Copper Clay

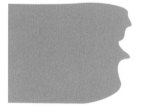

"Luscious and rich, hot reds bring an undeniable shot of life into any interior, whether the space is naturally dark or light. Powerful shades of deepest red, with their suggestion of fire and heat, bring an elemental quality to a room that cannot be ignored. These connotations of warmth make red the perfect shade for focal points around fireplaces and hearths." ABRAHAM & THAKORE

redcurrant

The devilishly rich shades of redcurrant comprise the fruity tones of cherry and tomato, through to a crop of crimson colors such as poppy and scarlet that are enriching and life-affirming. You cannot help but feel welcome in a hallway or living room that is bathed in reflected red tones that are instantly warming, noisy, and noticeable. Redcurrant is a great hit in northern climates, where its natural heat detracts from a lack of bright light. It will disguise a small space by making it feel enclosed but not claustrophobic, while in dining rooms rich reds stimulate conversation. The Chinese say that we should all have an accent of red in the house from which to gain energy; they associate it with good luck and fortune. This can take the form of a vase of red roses or vibrant red berries, or a statement ruby red wall around a fireplace or framing a comfortable sofa. However you use it, the redcurrant palette is fun and enriching, an uplifting shade that reassures as it warms a space.

Redcurrant paired with the night and day shades of white, black, or gray never fails to impress, giving a crisp but not cold combination of colors that sings with confidence and clarity. Before rushing to the paint pot, however, consider how much red you plan to use in a room. It is a color that doesn't sit too happily with other shades not directly related to it and works best with subtle oranges, pinks, or purples if used in a multi-layered color story.

1 Racing Red
2 Charcoal
3 Paprika
4 Tuscan Pink
5 Salmon White
6 Strawberry Milkshake

feel the heat In a contemporary Indian home,
New Delhi fashion designers Abraham & Thakore employ audacious
amounts of red. The red-pink sheer curtains and a gloss finish on the floor
and table allow the light to dance around the space and prevent the red
from becoming overpowering. Slate gray and black act as counterpoints.

marrakesh express
Moroccan architect Karim el Achak uses enriching red on the smooth flat surface of a wall, where it absorbs light and creates mellow tones. Redcurrant works well with shades of fuchsia, eggplant, and sunny yellow.

hot coals
In another Karim el Achak interior the combination of rich red and deep slate gray is both sleek and reassuring. A stainless steel flue and berber rugs plus brass Moroccan artifacts inject color and texture into a contemporary living room.

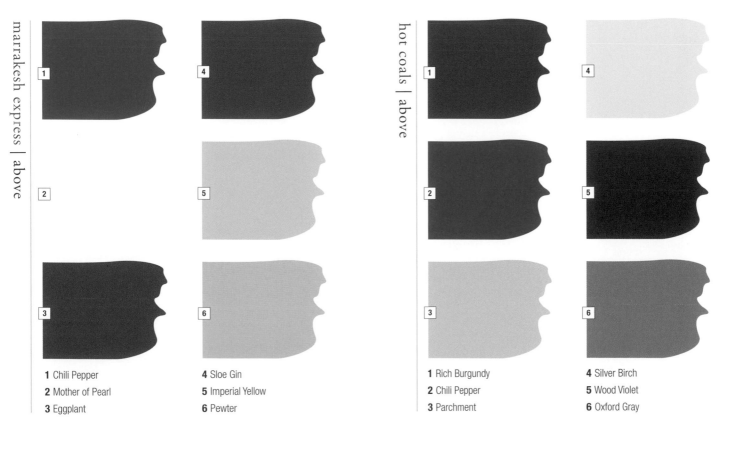

marrakesh express | above

1
2
3
4
5
6

1 Chili Pepper
2 Mother of Pearl
3 Eggplant
4 Sloe Gin
5 Imperial Yellow
6 Pewter

hot coals | above

1
2
3
4
5
6

1 Rich Burgundy
2 Chili Pepper
3 Parchment
4 Silver Birch
5 Wood Violet
6 Oxford Gray

lilac
& plum

grape
fig
blueberry
plum pie
radicchio
blackberry
boysenberry
deep purple
swiss chard
violet petal
sloe gin
bougainvillea
purple heart
crème de cassis
lavender blue
lilac
iris
french hydrangea
mauve sunset
vintage claret
rich ruby
magenta
marshmallow
misty rose
rioja
cyclamen
princess pink
passion flower
blush
sugar almond
umbrian rose
electric pink
tearose
crocus

ALL ABOUT PURPLE

Purple is all about power and passion. Its strong and versatile hues are associated with creativity, individualism, and inventiveness, perhaps by virtue of its changeable nature. Sitting between blue and red on the color wheel, it speaks volumes and is not for the fainthearted or timid, as it is strident and symbolic. It ranges from amethyst and deep purple velvet tones to the faded fresco colors of light lilac or lavender. Purple can surprise and delight in equal measure. It is an enriching palette, whether it warms a space with tones so deep they are almost black in their intensity, or whether it projects light around a space through light-hearted lavenders and lacy lilacs that may be pale in tone, yet still add significant richness to a room by bathing it in a warm, subtle glow.

At the serious end of the spectrum, eggplant is chic, solemn, and über-adult. It often works best as a rich accent, but a room bathed in purple is quite dramatic and surprisingly easy to live with, compared to some other strong colors. This deep velvety hue is a signature color for French designers Michael Coorengel and Jean-Pierre Calvagrac, who love the way it reflects their combined passions for the baroque and the contemporary. They often use it on all four walls of a room and combine it with a quite startling analogous shade of rich coral.

The many shades of purple are uplifting yet calming; they are spiritual colors that promote innovation and warm a space. The Japanese associate purple with wealth and social standing, while in Egypt purple denotes virtue and faith. And, of course, purple is the main papal color in the Vatican, closely related to both religion and serious ceremony. Purple has links with nobility. To be "born to the purple" is to be born into a royal or noble family.

Purple is emboldened by red and blue, made delicate by an association with white, or enveloped in passion by glossy finishes. It is a color that is not afraid to talk out loud and takes strident steps by raising the color temperature of a room.

The summery shades of pale lilac and lavender breathe light into dark spaces and a hint of sunshine into light ones. Although cheerful, these tones are astonishingly tricky to pin down. Always select a color several shades lighter than the one you are aiming for, as they are more powerful when applied. Violet is the color with the shortest wavelength on the spectrum, so it absorbs light easily. When viewed in sunny conditions it will appear more vivid and brighter in tone; artificial light will make it appear darker. Blue-tinged lilacs veer towards grayer colors, while red-tinged violets edge towards fuchsia.

Purple has always been a popular color in the garden, where it has a calming effect and makes small gardens seem larger. Its natural affinity with whites, off-whites, linens, and wheat tones outdoors translate well to the interior. Combining purples with these neutrals and introducing analogous tones of reds—whether vibrant or softer, pinker tones—together with blues in the form of denim or indigo creates really interesting palettes. Such combinations often linger in the visual memory thanks to their innate freshness and vitality.

Purple is more inviting than frightening. A powerful color, it denotes power and justice, regal connections, and a smart front. Purples are passionate, both romantic and seriously smart, and never go far out of fashion.

LILAC GRAY

FIG

"Lilac is one of my all-time favorite colors. I have incorporated its dreamy tones in my Denim fabric collection and even use it as a nail color. Sanderson Paint's French Lilac is the most perfect shade for creating a warm and inviting bedroom or living room." LENA PROUDLOCK

IRIS

BOYSENBERRY

MARSHMALLOW

SLOE GIN

USING PURPLE Purple is one of the most fascinating palettes to play with because it is so complex and versatile. It can be changeable in the paler tones, but in the solid, deeper tones it is a reassuring shade that anchors a space. Deep purples and pinks will definitely look better with a sheen, whereas a flat finish works well for the lighter shades.

Lavender reflects light really well so it is often used in rooms in northern Europe because it has a cheerful edge to it, even in the depths of winter. It can be deceptively strong, even in its paler shades, so experiment by applying it to a piece of lining paper and fix it to a wall where you want it to be. Watch it change throughout the course of a day before settling on a particular shade.

Geranium, in the very middle of the spectrum, is really most at home where the sun is strong, just like the flower itself. Hot pinky purples are a sure-fire way of grabbing the eye, so use them as accents or if you don't mind having this saturated shade center stage, then combine it with soft tones of cream or gray to divert attention elsewhere. Team it with acid green for a florid finish, but only use the green in small quantities; otherwise, you will just succeed in jarring your senses.

Other shades that go well with purples include browns, grays, and off-whites in all tints and tones. Reddish lilacs are quite geranium and pinky in tone, while bluish pale lilacs will head towards the gray end of the spectrum and become almost seascape in mood, giving a more ethereal feel and palette that is bluer overall.

Living rooms always look smart bathed in or accented by purple, as do dining rooms. Employ a full range of accent colors such as off-whites, wheats, grays, golds, and browns for a smart finish. Purple's complementary partners range from shimmery gilt at the eggplant end of the spectrum through to acid green for geranium and lilac or yellow at the violet side of things. There is no denying that the analogous combination of purple and pink is a powerful and popular one, if a little too strong for many people's tastes. Though gently done, in a way that apes the shades of pinky purple found in a garlic clove, this combination can produce a pleasing, not too punchy palette. While lilac and acid green can be quite slick if combined carefully, be watchful not to make too lurid a link by knocking back the brightness of the colors a little.

Kitchens, hallways, and bedrooms all look good lined with lilac, especially when such rooms have a nice supply of natural (but not necessarily bright or strong) light. Deep purples are best for dining rooms and living rooms, as well as bedrooms if you are feeling bold, as this color will raise the emotional heat slightly. Children always appreciate rooms that are suffused with fun, bright colors, especially those from the geranium palette, while sunny garden rooms look great when decorated with lilac walls, white flowers, and greenery, or emboldened with one wall painted in a hot pink geranium color. The more muted and reflective purple tones of gray-lavender, pale fig, and peony sit well in any cozy, relaxing space.

Serene and interesting in living spaces, calm and contemplative in bedrooms, colors in the purple spectrum are equally at home in restful spaces as they are in dining and entertaining areas, appearing quiet or bold depending on the setting.

OPPOSITE TOP LEFT This rich lacquered eggplant wall provides a glamorous backdrop to a transparent bar top that, lit from above, creates dramatic shafts of light.

OPPOSITE TOP RIGHT A fabulous wall of hot pink paint embraces this outdoor eating space with inviting shades of warm color in a modern Mexican setting.

OPPOSITE BOTTOM This bold scheme relies on the close relationship of analogous lilacs and blues. It consists of deep purple-blue walls that provide a tonal backdrop for canvases painted in royal blue, cornflower blue, and white, alongside bed drapes in a soft powder blue.

lilac & plum | parma violet

lilac & plum | geranium

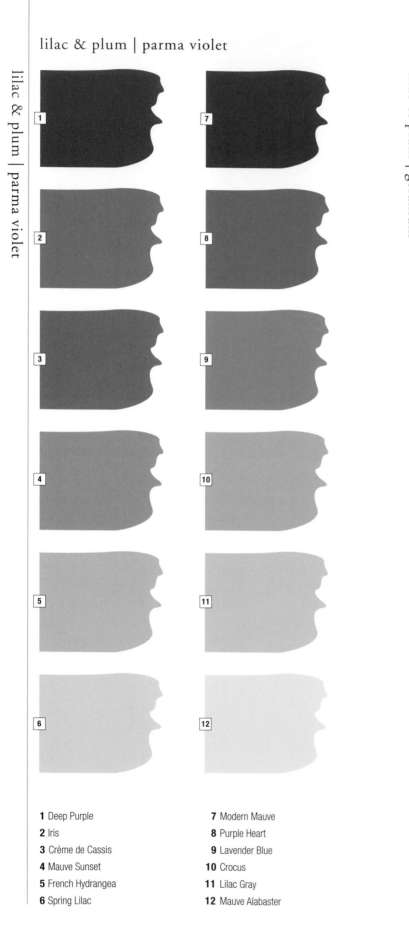

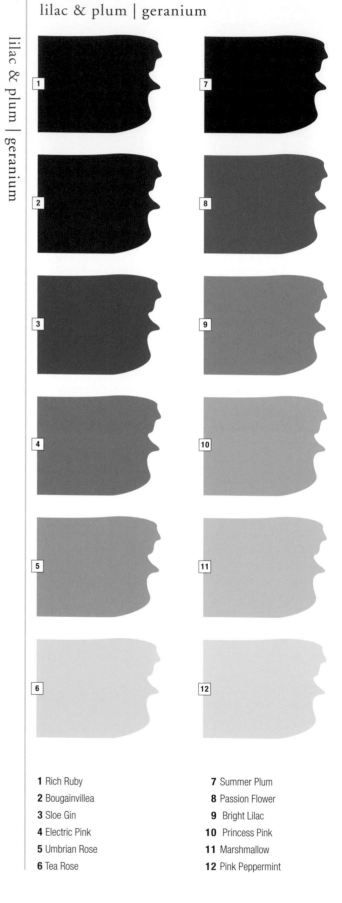

1 Deep Purple	**7** Modern Mauve	**1** Rich Ruby	**7** Summer Plum
2 Iris	**8** Purple Heart	**2** Bougainvillea	**8** Passion Flower
3 Crème de Cassis	**9** Lavender Blue	**3** Sloe Gin	**9** Bright Lilac
4 Mauve Sunset	**10** Crocus	**4** Electric Pink	**10** Princess Pink
5 French Hydrangea	**11** Lilac Gray	**5** Umbrian Rose	**11** Marshmallow
6 Spring Lilac	**12** Mauve Alabaster	**6** Tea Rose	**12** Pink Peppermint

ABOVE French designers Michael Coorengel and Jean-Pierre Calvagrac take inspiration from both contemporary and baroque interiors. White cornice detailing and painted furniture allow the deep eggplant tones to come to the forefront.

The color purple ranges from the deep, strong eggplant shades at the powerful blue end of the story, through vivid geranium and hot pinky purples to the delicate shades of lilac and lavender where reds enter the palette.

1 Blueberry

2 Fig

3 Plum Pie

4 Faded Grape

5 French Gray

6 Violet Petal

7 Grape

8 Boysenberry

9 Melrose Pink

10 Cranberry Ice

11 Countryside Pink

12 Misty Rose

"Using purple with a pink edge adds feminine glamour and sophistication, which brightens up any room. These colors are enjoyable even on overcast days, and create a sense of nobility and independence. Dark purple is associated with royalty, dignity, and transformation. Mixing in pink tones adds a hint of healing, femininity, and sweetness." JOHNNY GREY

parma violet

Lilac is best suffused with light so that its changeable nature can be fully appreciated. Versatile and interesting, the palest lilac that looks like only one or two shades from a pale gray can look barely there one minute and then, with the addition of generous natural sunlight or bright daylight, will transmute into glorious lavender tones that are at once feminine and flattering. This is why when you are choosing a lilac color it is really important to go several shades lighter than your intended color, otherwise you will end up with a vile shade of tasteless mauve that will send shudders through your room. To prove the point, take a tear sheet of a room whose lilac color you like and match it to a paint chart. It is always surprising with lilac just how terribly pale you have to go to get the right result. Lilac, when it is used in exactly the right way, can be light-enhancing and delicate rather than bright and brash. For inspiration, consider the appealing shades of old-fashioned parma violets, the pinky blue of the hydrangea head, and the richer tones of a Provençal lavender field. Vital and uplifting, these soft shades are perfectly pinkish, but not cloying.

Use lilacs in kitchens and hallways to appreciate how much their colors vary throughout the day. They work well in bedrooms, too, bringing a fresh and sunny atmosphere with them, even in northern light. Essentially spring and summer colors, lilacs are nevertheless perfectly pleasing year round.

THIS PAGE Hilton McConnico's Paris apartment is a symphony in lilac without being overpowering. Fresh, clean tones of parma violet on walls, curtains, and even candelabras are punchy and inviting. A dark wooden floor provides a good counterpoint.

OPPOSITE This tranquil and inviting bedroom was decorated to complement a series of color field paintings in the home of Nicholas Alvis Vega and Liza Bruce. Three harmonious tones of parma violet, pale mauve, and deep lilac, applied in horizontal bands from dark to light, demonstrate just how much natural light these colors absorb. The paler tones almost merge into the darker shades where the light is brightest.

multi-layered
In a house designed by Don Chapell, kitchen units are painted in a subtle color palette of sea greens, soft rosy earth, and pale lilacs. Each of the shades relates to the tones and hues found in the surrounding landscape in Sarasota, Florida.

kitchen zing
Sharp citrus lime chimes well against a wall of lavender and kitchen cabinets in pale-toned beech wood in a classic case of how the right accent color can bring both definition and visual interest to a palette.

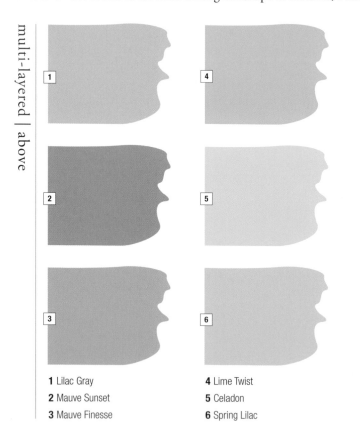

multi-layered | above

1 Lilac Gray
2 Mauve Sunset
3 Mauve Finesse
4 Lime Twist
5 Celadon
6 Spring Lilac

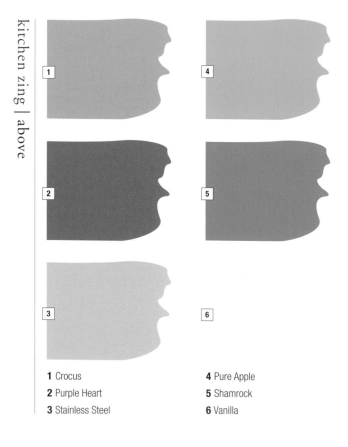

kitchen zing | above

1 Crocus
2 Purple Heart
3 Stainless Steel
4 Pure Apple
5 Shamrock
6 Vanilla

cool dining
At the opposite end of the kitchen shown top left on the opposite page, a dining area is painted in the same color but in differing proportions to provide a lively eating space. Beech dining chairs and shades ranging from deep purple to pale lavender combine to make the mood sharp, fresh, and fun.

1 Lavender Blue
2 Cornflower Blue
3 Mint Tea
4 Barley
5 Fig
6 Sunset

"Floral, exciting, powerful, alive, positive, and really uplifting—use strong geranium shades with electric oranges or lime green for a perfectly complementary story or calm the space with pure whites and silver highlights. Always optimistic and pleasurable, geranium is a rich color that enhances white spaces and adds soft warmth to small rooms."   KARIM RASHID

THIS PAGE A dress handmade by artist Nathalie Lete hangs on one wall of her Parisian bedroom, where strong panels of pink and burgundy help create a faintly fifties look.

OPPOSITE Premium pink walls absorb strong natural daylight and provide a rich counterpoint to a reflective gray zinc work surface and shelving in Mexico.

geranium

Geranium embraces the reddish tones of purple and the hot pinky tones of red to create a vivid spectrum that includes fuchsia and bougainvillea. In hot countries it works beautifully on walls; in cooler climates, use it with care and vary the shades so one color doesn't dominate. Fuchsia accents look strong but not overpowering in neutral spaces.

U.S. designer Jamie Drake often employs hot pinks on walls and accessories—indeed it is one of his favorite colors. Such strong tones can work very successfully when limited to one wall of a room. Combine them with dusky gray-pinks to add a layer of subtlety and prevent the pink from grabbing all the attention. And use further analogous shades of amethyst and intense purples to provide drama and gravitas. Combine geranium with steely grays as a foil for the brightness, or keep the story fresh by adding in rose-tinged whites and pearly off-whites. For sheer fun, you can use geranium shades on walls in the garden, where they will be absorbed by the sun and provide a suitably lush backdrop for a panoply of rich greenery.

In bathrooms geranium is a particularly successful color, as its pink/red tones will enhance your skin tone and therefore improve how you feel when you view yourself in the mirror each morning. Rich shades on the walls here are capable of setting your mood for the day, so don't be afraid to embrace the feminine in the bathroom.

casa viva | right

1 Rich Ruby
2 Electric Pink
3 Pine Sprigs
4 Pink Peppermint
5 Blue Orchid
6 Mighty Aphrodite

casa viva

A serene, all-white bed is canopied in deep pink sheer fabric and backed by a deep raspberry crush wall that provides strong definition in the room as well as anchoring the bed. Pink-tinged gray flooring and a sherbet-colored contemporary day bed nod to the red end of the spectrum, while still providing contrast.

74   LILAC & PLUM

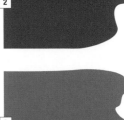

rich in pink A Manhattan apartment bathed in designer Jamie Drake's strong signature colors is unmistakeably glamorous and appealing. The color cue for the dining room scheme comes from the painting, all of whose colors are represented somewhere in the room, whether in the decoration or the furniture and accessories.

1 Electric Pink
2 Rich Ruby
3 Bright Lilac
4 Cheetah
5 Blueberry
6 Silver Mink

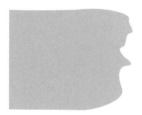

"Farrow & Ball Pelt No. 254 is rich plum-brown, lighter and less red than Farrow & Ball's Brinjal, but with the same dramatic effect; it has something of the natural tones of dark animal fur. Pelt is incredibly versatile and will change dramatically in effect and impact when contrasted with other colors and when used in varying lights." SARAH COLE, DIRECTOR, FARROW & BALL

eggplant

OPPOSITE Dado-height panels of deep plum topped with a thin stripe of royal red provide a rich and subtle anchor for an otherwise minimally furnished bedroom.

Dark purple can make a room appear larger than life, making the walls and ceiling disappear, so is a good color to use in small spaces. It is also good for creating intimacy, so is equally at home in cozy living spaces as it is in romantic bedrooms. If the thought of rooms bathed in purple seems too much, then consider using it sparingly, by applying it below dado height or on just one wall, then add in smaller elements such as vases or pillows, throws, and lampshades. Deep purples lend themselves to glossy and reflective surfaces, so use them on velvets and silk drapes and upholstery as well as on softly glossy walls. This is the one color that does not work quite so well when applied in matte, murky shades.

Purple blues such as rich midnight and deepest cobalt are seriously sexy colors that are just right in dining rooms that call for smart evening entertaining. Introduce some glossy gilt tones in the form of mirrors or shimmering glassware and add in some soft lighting and you will succeed in creating a touch of Hollywood glamour and a perfect mood.

Living rooms always look smart bathed in or accented by purple, while kitchens, hallways, and bedrooms prefer lilac or geranium shades. Children's rooms, which always enjoy bright colors, will benefit from purple, and sunny garden rooms look great suffused with lilac walls, white flowers, and greenery.

THIS PAGE Deep eggplant walls make a handsome color story together with faded olive and oak steel-framed vintage canteen dining chairs.

regal elegance

Deep purple combined with vivid cranberry red and turquoise green accents, plus white counterpoints on picture frames and a freestanding sculpture, demonstrate how a successful palette can work using clashing colors.

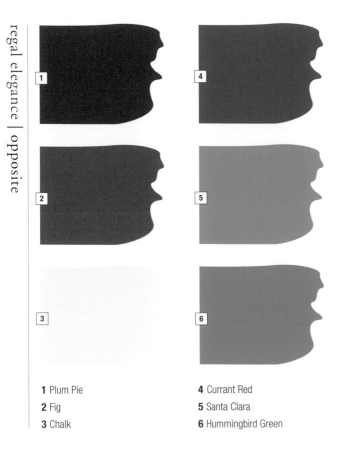

1 Plum Pie
2 Fig
3 Chalk

4 Currant Red
5 Santa Clara
6 Hummingbird Green

Deep purple enriches a space, providing a backdrop for shades of gilt, olive, and vivid reds. It is a color that works in small spaces and larger rooms, in contemporary and traditional settings.

reading room

This kitchen and living area has storage space disguised behind deep plum, push-catch sectioned closets that provide an interesting glossy color panel while doubling up as a space divider within the room.

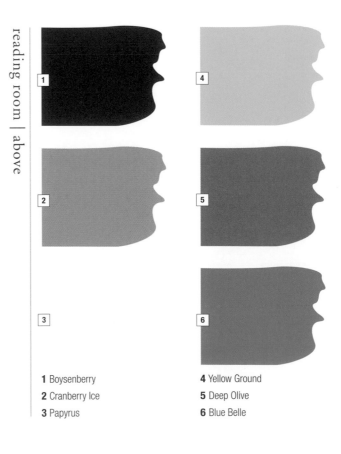

1 Boysenberry
2 Cranberry Ice
3 Papyrus

4 Yellow Ground
5 Deep Olive
6 Blue Belle

sea & sky

hibiscus
rockpool
azure
seaspray
cornflower
shoreline
mexico
duck egg
indigo
caribbean
midnight blue
wedgwood
beach shack
steely sky
kingfisher
mediterranean
denim
sapphire
ultramarine
prussian blue
turquoise
lapis
delft
bayberry
riviera
powder blue
gustavian
aquamarine
shaker blue
periwinkle
hawaiian sea
cobalt
milori blue
forget-me-not

ALL ABOUT BLUE

Blue denotes comfort, security, and peacefulness. It is everywhere in nature and therefore suits us well. The blue palette evokes the sea and the sky, with calm elemental colors that lend watery tones and nautical connotations to an interior. Blue is versatile, whether with the cooler hues of sky and duck egg or the interesting, mysterious blue-grays that may verge on the slightly austere, but are nevertheless soulful and graceful.

Basing palettes on the naturally occurring colors of the coastal path always produces a pleasing result, as whenever you reproduce one of nature's palettes, the colors always work. They feel at home with one another. Think of wheat grass swaying wistfully against a stormy sky, melancholic seaspray lapping against clam shells on a pebble beach, or mottled ocher sand against a pale fall sky. These are the ethereal sea and sky colors that are contemplative yet easy on the eye, creating an instant sense of calmness and well-being.

At the brighter end of the spectrum vivid tones of cobalt and turquoise are joyous colors, most at home in southern climates, where the strong sunlight brings out their rich hues and keeps them looking bright but not garish. They need the sun to bring out their deep color. In the northern hemisphere they can look very cold, so use the stronger shades of denim, periwinkle, and jewel-bright turquoise or aquamarine as accents for maximum impact without overkill. These are powerful, enriching shades when used with restraint.

Florida, California, and Mexico are the perfect settings for strong blues, but further north they only really work as accent colors, turquoise especially. In Europe, and particularly in the U.K., it is best to "dirty up" blue tones to soften them and give them warmth. Duck egg and pale Provençal blue look wonderful here when they have just enough gray and burnt umber in them to dull their sheen. Elusive and delicate, the elegant tones of duck egg and teal work in the same way as a filigree fretwork screen provides elegant tracery in a space—they allow light to subtly bounce around and create a soft, clear sheen around a room. Think of 18th-century Gustavian interiors from Sweden.

The classic crisp navy and white nautical palette, so often used in bathrooms, shower rooms, and seaside living spaces, always looks fresh and appealing, although it is best to choose some creamy, dreamy off-whites to accompany true navy. They are still crisp-looking but somehow more inviting than pure white. Mix in some linen colors too, such as shades of gray fisherman's rope or jute, to soften the atmosphere.

Sky tones include elegant Wedgwood blue, which works well punctuated with a shot of red for a fresh, lively bedroom. Or tone it down with a knocked-back white, like the china itself, for an elegant but warm result.

From the classic combination of china blue and ice white to delicate shades of egg shell and seaspray, blue is uplifting and refreshing, harmonious and welcoming.

Blue's complementary color, yellow, works best when tweaked along the color spectrum away from too vivid a sunflower yellow if it will be combined with a strong shade of blue. From pale sand at one end to an enriching ocher at the other, this is a good range in which to form a palette. The overused combination of bright blue and bright yellow, while an enduring classic and a combination that was frequently used in many kitchens in the late seventies, looks a little tired. It's far more exciting to experiment at the paler end of the spectrum. Blue and white has often been a color theme for kitchens, thanks to the blue and white china traditions extending from Chinese to Wedgwood and Cornishware.

MEXICO

AQUAMARINE

POOLSIDE

"There is something about the color blue. Perhaps it is the primeval influence of the vast daytime sky or the deep sea. Perhaps it is the enormous range of colors commonly considered to be blue. From intense navy blue and royal blue to the subtlety of baby blue and cerulean, from the deep velvet of a night sky to the lagoons of the Caribbean, there is a blue for every taste." CARL MINCHEW,

DIRECTOR OF COLOR TECHNOLOGY, BENJAMIN MOORE

COBALT

GUNMETAL BLUE

MILITARY UNIFORM

Blue never fails to enliven the spirit and lift the soul. Popular and peaceful, it is the perfect weekend color, promoting calm and recuperation.

USING BLUE Blue is the signature color for many a room. It is capable of being bright and breezy, moody and elusive, or deep and mysterious, depending on the range of shades used. One of the most popular colors around, it invariably refreshes and revives the senses.

Sea and sky colors range from the pale blue-grays of driftwood and leaden seascapes to crisp, clear summer skies and the turquoise glory of a Caribbean ocean to deep stormy midnight blues, almost as black as night.

The Shakers often used a shade of blue named Heavenly Blue that is a cross between a deep Provençal cornflower blue and navy. It was used to paint furniture and on woodwork and always looked crisp against the wheaten tones of handcrafted pine furniture. Heavenly indeed.

Shipshape and nautical, classical blue and white schemes in which the paler colors provide accents veer from the Cornishware blue and cream to the ever popular navy and white stripes of Breton vests and the sharp maritime navy that tones so well with true white. While a strictly nautical scheme can be somewhat predictable and perhaps a little cold, it is interesting to steer

Use the nautical palette as a starting point but shift the color boundaries to create new partners—turquoise and imperial yellow, sky blue and coral, powder blue and biscotti.

the combination in different directions for slightly more adventurous results. Ralph Lauren has made the nautical palette his own by taking a subtle approach to maritime associations and using pencil-thin navy lines on ticking fabrics against antique white walls. The result is a restrained coastal style that always looks fresh.

Sky blues, for instance, make good partners for steely gray whites, as well as their perfect partners of sand and corn shades that lend a fresh, summery, and coastal edge. Blue taken to a semi-turquoise level will appear elegant against ice-white architectural detailing or upholstery. Accent this with a striking imperial yellow and you will see a jewel-like contrast that will pop with life. Silver and gold work wonders against pale blues, bringing a sharp edge and reflective planes that enrich the clear tones of the blue.

Denim blues or those that look best in matte, chalky tones such as moody gray-blues work well in bathrooms, especially so when combined with dusky pinks that have a strong element of red. Or use coral for a softer accent.

The rich and more vibrant ocean shades of azure, periwinkle, or aqua require more sensitive handling. Team them with dark wood shades rather than pure white to best effect. Watery, rockpool blues always work with iridescent surfaces, so think about introducing shimmery silk fabrics, china, or glass that plays with the light or some sleek, glossy silvery blues in the form of blue-on-blue tones. Experiment with two tones of wall color, blue accents in the form of pillows, and let the colors create a harmonious collection of shades that meld into one another.

OPPOSITE TOP LEFT Perfect sky blue walls are both fresh and restful. Here they make a calming palette combined with furniture and a bedhead in sandy shades designed by Bill Mostow.

OPPOSITE TOP RIGHT Seascape colors include moody sky tones as well as uplifting brights. In Agnès Emery's Moroccan house, slate-blue–painted furniture has a subtle quality, changing tones as sunlight moves around the house throughout the day.

OPPOSITE BOTTOM LEFT Designers Carlos Mota and Miles Redd have employed a succulent royal blue to create a cozy intimacy in this period living room in New York.

OPPOSITE BOTTOM RIGHT Undersea tones collide in a watery-inspired mix of Caribbean blue and sunny aqua in this bedroom scheme.

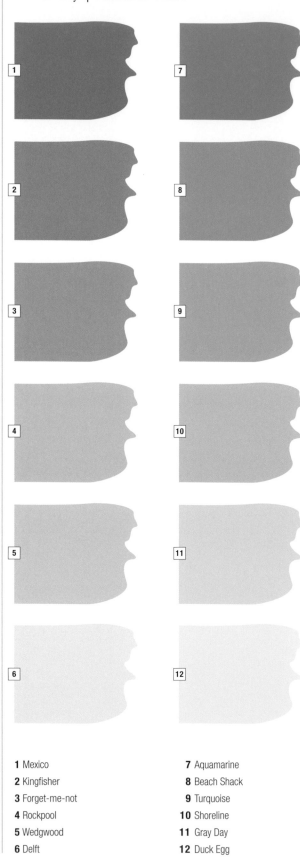

Sea and sky colors are some of the most popular, uplifting and endlessly variable tones used to decorate with. Strong, calming, and trustworthy, they are dependable but not dull, dynamic but not overpowering.

ABOVE This neutral scheme is defined and completed with a painted French window in duck egg blue, and one wall painted in an ethereal sky blue to provide impact, warmth, and depth in an otherwise understated space.

1 Mexico	**7** Aquamarine
2 Kingfisher	**8** Beach Shack
3 Forget-me-not	**9** Turquoise
4 Rockpool	**10** Shoreline
5 Wedgwood	**11** Gray Day
6 Delft	**12** Duck Egg

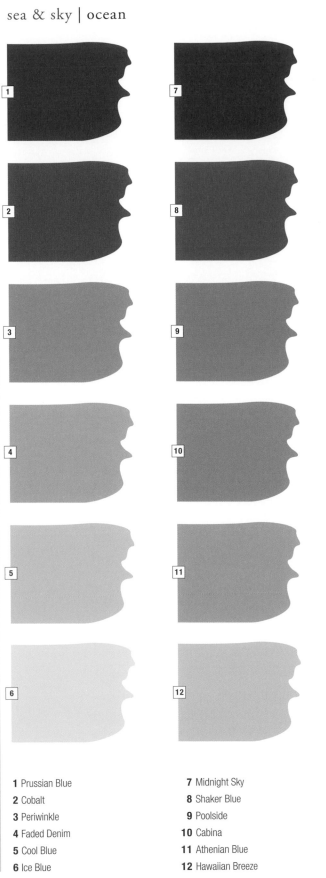

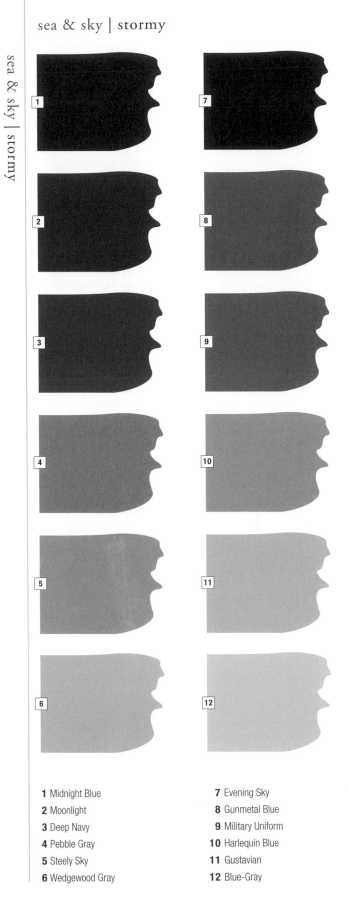

1 Prussian Blue

2 Cobalt

3 Periwinkle

4 Faded Denim

5 Cool Blue

6 Ice Blue

7 Midnight Sky

8 Shaker Blue

9 Poolside

10 Cabina

11 Athenian Blue

12 Hawaiian Breeze

1 Midnight Blue

2 Moonlight

3 Deep Navy

4 Pebble Gray

5 Steely Sky

6 Wedgewood Gray

7 Evening Sky

8 Gunmetal Blue

9 Military Uniform

10 Harlequin Blue

11 Gustavian

12 Blue-Gray

"Ralph Lauren's River Rapids WHO3B is white with the palest tint of blue. I used it on the interior walls of my cabinets in the dining room. My collection of old silver shimmers off of it. It is very similar to the background color of my blue and white Chinese export china. It is also the perfect color for a ceiling in a brown or white room." ALEX BATES, WEST ELM

summer skies

THIS PAGE Crisp, clean cornflower blue set against pale primrose and a warm white delights the eyes and senses with a summery feel.

OPPOSITE Palest sky blue is heightened by shafts of natural light that bounce around the room and evoke sunny days by the coast.

Summer sky blue is often mistaken as a cold color, but as long as it has a certain amount of magenta or purple in its base it can be wonderfully soft, warming, and uplifting, especially in bedrooms and living rooms.

Keeping blues warm is a matter of applying a shade that has warm tones in it and teaming it with rich, sandy shades that echo the seashore, or else crisp whites, cool grays, and palest yellows. Pale clear blue also looks fabulous combined with red-toned oak or chestnut furniture, which serves to keep the atmosphere warm rather than cool.

White is the perfect foil for this color as it mimics the summer skyline, bringing freshness to a summery palette. Provide shots of additional color by adding tomato red or acid green accents in the form of flowers, fabrics, or china for extra zing. The classic combination of blue and white is a perennial favorite and is endlessly adaptable. Cornish blue and cream, Greek Island sky and ice white, pale topaz and buttermilk are all variations on a classic core palette that shift subtly yet produce transforming nuances in a palette. The key to success is to use soft off-whites that have a touch of magenta or gray so the white is not too punchy; otherwise, you risk bringing out the coldness in the blue.

These colors and combinations are adaptable enough to suit any room, from bedrooms to kitchens. They work best in spaces that benefit from generous natural light, but can survive in both the north and the south.

rich wood
Earth tones of oak wood ground an ethereal pale blue in a smart dining area, while accents of reddish pink and sand warm up the space. Pale blue and wood, ranging from light beech to deep mahogany, is a winning combination.

manhattan cool
Busts on pedestals provide white contrast in this library and dining room in a New York apartment, where jewel-like accents of warm lime and bright turquoise, together with lilac alliums, are set against Wedgwood blue walls.

rich wood | above

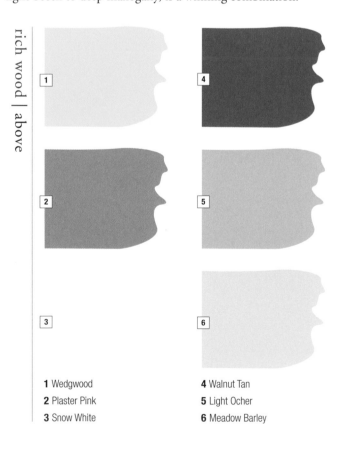

manhattan cool | above

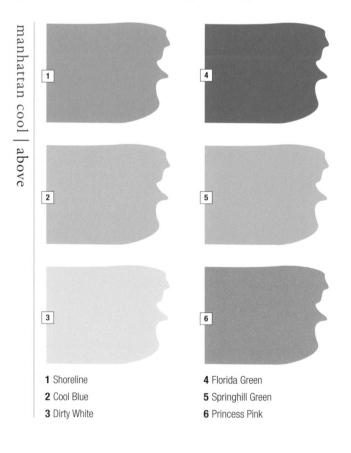

1 Wedgwood

2 Plaster Pink

3 Snow White

4 Walnut Tan

5 Light Ocher

6 Meadow Barley

1 Shoreline

2 Cool Blue

3 Dirty White

4 Florida Green

5 Springhill Green

6 Princess Pink

provençal dining Clear-toned

walls and white woodwork provide a fresh backdrop to this sunny
area for dining and entertaining. Red and pink counterpoints on the
multi-patterned seat covers and the accessories complete this
understated nautical scheme of blue, white, and red.

1 Rockpool
2 Kingfisher
3 Blue-Gray
4 Ladybug Red
5 Genuine Pink
6 Moroccan Red

china corner

Everyone loves blue and white rooms. Charming baby blue walls are a perfect complementary statement for the creamware pitchers and classic country blue-and-white tableware displayed on a painted dresser. Accent tones in wheaten gray, rich buttermilk, and gunmetal gray also sit well together.

china corner | opposite

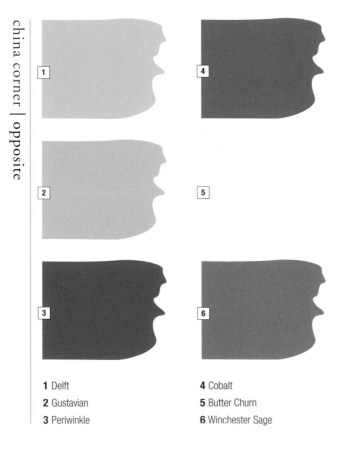

1 Delft
2 Gustavian
3 Periwinkle

4 Cobalt
5 Butter Churn
6 Winchester Sage

Invigorating and informal, the summer skies palette is just right for coastal settings and anywhere that needs a cheery uplift. Shades ranging from lilac-blue to rich Wedgwood blue-gray all work well.

coastal calm

Powder blue woodwork on the chair and cabinet doors, sky blue and deeper gray walls, and a glossy floor of biscuit tones are defined and edged with plain white woodwork and punctuated with redcurrant red on the towel and hints of hyacinth. This is truly a crisp and easy-living palette for sea lovers everywhere.

coastal calm | above

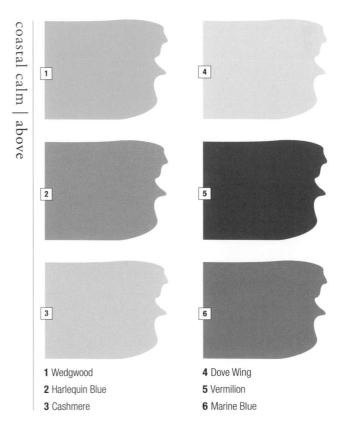

1 Wedgwood
2 Harlequin Blue
3 Cashmere

4 Dove Wing
5 Vermilion
6 Marine Blue

"The one element to consider when you choose your palette is the style and period of the building and, more importantly, its geographical context (urban or country, climate, natural light). For example, the summery blue I chose as a dominant color for my house in Marrakesh was not chosen because we are near the sea. This is the exact shade that is offered in the streets of the medina." AGNÈS EMERY, EMERY & CIE

ocean

The denim and azure colors of deep royal blue and deep watery greeny blues are persistently popular colors to decorate with. The Caribbean-inspired turquoise and azures are often the colors that are craved in wintery northern light, but they really do not work there. What looks fabulous on a Caribbean vacation does not readily translate to a London or New York home. Jewel-like aqua may sit happily in a Bahamas living space, but it in fact needs strong sun to appear so alive. In the north it would simply seem cold and out of place.

Vivid royal blues, inspired by the Mediterranean sea colors, look wonderful pared with matte chalky, "sad" grays, which provide a calming counterpoint. Or use them in a workspace, studio, or home office against linen white woodwork for a punchy, uplifting space. On the other hand, denim and electric blues are perfect for those places where the light is not bright. Because they look dirtied up, with elements of chalky gray or earth tones as part of their core color, they absorb light and change with the quality of the light over the course of the day or when placed under artificial light. This mutability will make it seem as though the walls are "talking" to you. These tones are perfect for making a strong color statement in a dining area or a kitchen, used as a wall color against pale beech or ash cupboards. In fact, they work well with wood of all tones, from limed oak to rich cherrywood.

THIS PAGE Deep tones of rich ocean blue on the walls are sharply complemented with smart contemporary lighting and office furniture in this home office in Helsinki designed by Ulla Koskinen. White woodwork and ceiling, together with a pale beech floor, break up the color and allow light to reflect off of it.

OPPOSITE In Agnès Emery's home in Marrakesh the kitchen is outdoors, so tiles are a practical way of introducing color. Vivid tiled walls in jewel-bright ocean tones provide a reflective surface for natural light, and merge well with matte gray-painted closets.

1 Prussian Blue
2 Winter Gates
3 Silver Birch
4 Secluded Beach
5 Noisette
6 Classic Brown

spanish modern This Ibizan retreat

designed by Ramón Esteve is bathed in natural light, painted

white with polished concrete floors, and furnished with iroko wood and

steel for ultimate cool living in a hot climate. Jolts of ocean blue on

one wall in several rooms allude to the sea that surrounds the house.

turquoise twist A moody fall-like

sea color is well counterpointed with shades of wheatgrass, weather-beaten sand, and red rocks. Quiet and contemplative, this is a good palette for a bedroom as it provides a calming atmosphere. Blues and browns are ever-present on coasts and along riverfronts, in differing intensities.

1 Athenian Blue
2 Delft
3 Ocher
4 Great White
5 Greenfield Pumpkin
6 Roxbury Caramel

"To create a soothing atmosphere in the dining room I used warm materials in deep shades of eggplant, gray, black, and taupe. This carefully chosen, rich palette was mixed to create an elegant room, with the bold shades adding elegance and interest. These shades are understated and subtle, which is why they recur in my interiors." LUIGI ESPOSITO

stormy

THIS PAGE Midnight blue walls and painted cabinets provide a receding backdrop in a bedroom where white bed linen and an oak bedside table provide the visual focus. Designer John Minshaw has put together an unusual but successful color palette for a bedroom.

OPPOSITE Designer Luigi Esposito has created a sense of glamour using a stormy night-sky palette that is particularly successful after dark, when the walls absorb any natural light in the room. The sparkling light from the chandeliers places the emphasis on the dining area.

Rich, exotic blues are undergoing a renaissance in home décor. These versatile deep shades make great bases and accents, and can be used in many tones and fabrics for everything from elegant to ethnic. Midnight blue is the decorators' favorite for night-time dining rooms. It is at its best with soft lighting, candles, gleaming silverware, and white table linen. For less formal rooms, midnight blue can be used as a background color to contrast with almost any hue—sugar plum pink and creamy whites; all the shades of pale to mid blues; and even sharp green.

The dark, stormy shades also team well with other blues and greens and earth tones, especially coffee shades. They can be used extensively in living areas and also make fine accent colors, particularly in the form of glass and china or sumptuous velvet drapes. As with all rich colors, experiment a little on a small area before you leap in, as it is important to assess the impact of such a dramatic color. Stormy blues work well in northern light; they have been dirtied up so don't need natural light to enhance the warmth.

It is hard to underestimate the importance of small contrasting colors that complement the main palette of a room. For instance, vibrant yellow flowers look wonderful with blue, or choose small sunflower pillows against navy upholstery for a jolt of interesting color. Unexpected fabrics on a dark oak table will lend a new level of interest, as will carefully chosen rugs.

1 Gunmetal Blue
2 Gunmetal
3 Silver Birch
4 Plum Pie
5 Ansonia Peach
6 Titanium White

wedgwood blues John Minshaw has
taken the classic darker Wedgwood blue and created a sophisticated palette
by combining it with a porcelain white, then accenting it with golden tones
in the form of gilt mirrors and gilt-edged historical portraits. A soft mauve
used on the upholstery of oak-framed chairs echoes the golds elsewhere.

gray skies

This Moroccan bathroom, designed by Paris-based Agnès Emery, is a story based around stormy sunrise and sunset tones—fierce mauve-oranges, steely gray clouds, and muddy blue tones. Ironically, moody colors produce a serene palette.

cool cuisine

In designer Axel Vervoordt's Belgium home the matte, stormy blues are confined to accents, used on ceiling beams, window frames, and painted chairs to give an overall impression of muted blue. The terra-cotta tiles provide warmth.

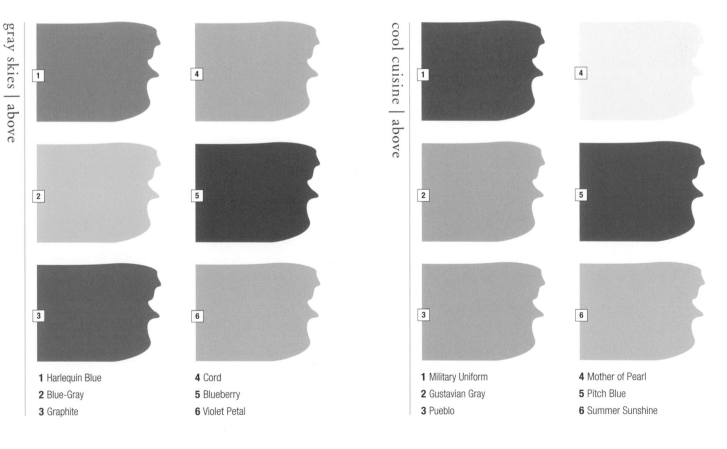

gray skies | above

1 Harlequin Blue
2 Blue-Gray
3 Graphite
4 Cord
5 Blueberry
6 Violet Petal

cool cuisine | above

1 Military Uniform
2 Gustavian Gray
3 Pueblo
4 Mother of Pearl
5 Pitch Blue
6 Summer Sunshine

avocado
& pistachio

emerald
jade
prickly pear
pine tree
endive
pine woods
cool mint
love bird
sage
cilantro
celadon
chameleon
khaki
zuccini
amazon
pear
lime twist
meadow
concombre
gothic green
herb garden
olive tree
mint tea
dew
chrome green
cooking apple
brunswick green
mint chocolate chip
forest
chicory tip
spring greens
moss
bramley
fern

ALL ABOUT GREEN

Green is popular right now, and for all the right reasons. Its close association with all things natural and sustainable means that it has made a big interiors comeback of late. From the pleasing translucent tones of pale celery and delicate pistachio to the reassuring lime and forest tones at the richer end of the spectrum, green provides nurture as well as nature. A relaxing, enriching, and comforting color, it symbolizes growth, harmony, and fertility.

As a secondary color formed by mixing blue and yellow, greens can be pushed to either ends of the spectrum. Yellowy-greens can be temperamental and not always easy to work with, as they are capable of looking sickly and unappealing in certain lights. It can sometimes be hard to pinpoint accurately a chosen shade at the yellow end of the palette, as all the more troublesome properties of yellow may apply. The solution may be to break up surfaces and combine a variety of shades.

Green is best used like an orchestra, as a sum of parts rather than a stand-alone color. It works best as part of a symphony, making its presence felt in separate, but cohesive elements that include wood, texture, and tone on tone. Think of all the greens in the yard or the forest and how lightweight leaves, such as ferns, reflect light through their tracery veins and become limey in tone, while thicker leaves and plants such as palms absorb the light and project deep racing green tones. Green is always a success when combined with woody tones and wood itself, from pale ash or beech to warm oak, pine, or wenge. Vivid shades of apple, pea, *Alchemilla mollis* and euphorbia both echo nature and create an instinctive complement to mocha and mahogany furniture or, indeed, brown-painted walls. A green that veers towards the blue end of the story always

Green, like its constituent blue, is said to have a wider emotional range than red or yellow.

warms walls and makes an uplifting statement. It is best combined with plain or painted wood rather than busy patterned upholstery or fabric elsewhere in the room.

As a heritage color, vivid pea green was a color closely associated with the 18th and 19th centuries both in Europe and across the United States. At first it was only the wealthy who could afford to use strong color, since the natural pigments used to create vivid paints were expensive and elusive. As cheaper formulations such as railing green and green verditer became available from the late 19th century onwards, so color moved to a broader social spectrum. Many of these traditional greens had a blue bias and remain popular today, particularly in Swedish-style interiors, where traditional schemes have always favored green-blues and blue-greens because they work well in limited northern light.

Green stands for growth, harmony, and peaceful reassurance. Green in nature has texture, but sometimes reproduces as a flat, cold tone on a wall. For warmth and depth, use a green that includes elements of burnt umber, red, or yellow ocher.

In Art Deco interiors and exteriors, mint greens were popular teamed with ice cream shades of cotton candy pink and noisette, while the Bloomsbury Literary Set in Charleston, their Sussex enclave, painted their rooms in many vivid hues, including a rich pea green. By the 1950s green had been toned down and was more understated.

Nowadays, the subtle tones of olive, moss, and khaki are finding favor with a generation for whom conservation and sustainable living are imperative. They team beautifully with fiery tangerine, sherbet lemon, and jolts of fuchsia or gilt to make an enriching environment.

APPLE LIME

MINT TEA

SAGE GREEN

"Earthy greens are calm and soothing, ranging from the brighter realms of Farrow & Ball's Churlish Green to the perfect accent shades of Ball Green and Vert de Terre. Greens have a natural affinity with earth colors, and provoke a pleasing counterpoint to soft lilac and muddy mauve tones."

SARAH COLE, DIRECTOR, FARROW & BALL

FOREST HILLS GREEN

FADED GREEN

CHAMELEON

USING GREEN What I call "spiritual green," the clean tones of celadon and celery, are at once feminine, elusive, and sophisticated. They add a subtle glamour wherever they are used but work particularly well in living rooms, bedrooms, and bathrooms. Combined with off-whites and deep mocha, this shade is an unbeatable color where you want to create a smart but subtle palette.

When choosing green palettes, make use of natural plants to help you choose a particular shade. The garden greens of foliage and leaves are great starting points for formulating a wider palette. Pick sprigs of *Alchemilla mollis* or lily-of-the-valley to create a color match for a no-nonsense range of leaf-inspired shades that are unmistakeably bright and breezy. Beware, though, that these richly-textured organic forms can sometimes be hard to replicate in green paint, which can, like yellow, be tricky to handle. Make sure you choose a green that has a substantial amount of red, yellow ocher, or burnt umber in its base. These shades are warmer and deeper. If the tone of green is wrong it can affect your mood. An acidic green applied to kitchen or bathroom walls, for instance, will reflect badly on your face and make you look unhealthy.

Where there is a lot of light it is better to use blue-green or cool greens and where the light is gray and dark, chose warm greens. Dark greens are restful and meditative, perfect for a study or a library. They work well with orange-red, crimson brown, and pink. Earthy greens look great with all browns. Think of how these tones work in nature when choosing shades to work with.

Green's opposite on the color wheel is red and this vibrant juxtaposition conjures such delicious combinations as tomatoes and basil, rosy red apples and green leaves, and fruits of the forest. Dirty greens and rich reds are a classic combination in traditional Swedish interiors, used on fabrics and painted furniture and woodwork, while Farrow & Ball's Cooking Apple Green is a lush, popular green that changes character according to light levels, becoming rich in sunlight and staying mellow in muted light.

It's best to experiment with understated greens before working up to bolder shades. Powerful greens on walls are capable of overpowering a space, whereas stronger tones on curtains and furnishings are less obtrusive.

Delicious accents for greens include rich russets teamed with sage green for subtle sophistication, and chocolate brown for a fashionable fix against faded lime or gentle pear. In living and dining areas greens are great for promoting relaxation and conversation, while in a kitchen pea green and salad shades are fresh and inviting, especially when combined with bright white, or buttercream for a slightly retro palette.

Using green as accents is particularly easy in kitchens and dining areas, where colored glasses and deep green china are perennial favorites. Think red wine in green glasses and radicchio leaves on green plates; natural contrasts that provide table decoration in their own right. Complete the setting with green napkins and a wall painted in palest celery or celadon and the symphony will display all the right harmonies.

OPPOSITE TOP LEFT This pale apple snug area provides peaceful pause for thought in a Moroccan riad created by Agnès Emery. She often uses tiles to produce color, decoration, texture, and interesting reflective surfaces in her energetic interiors.

OPPOSITE TOP RIGHT Exquisite celery green is at once elegant and enriching in this period dining room. Delicate accents are provided by chairs covered in toile de Jouy fabric, bone china edged in gold leaf, and a cinnamon-colored chandelier.

OPPOSITE BOTTOM Cool moss walls and a gray granite floor make a sophisticated statement, but shots of lemon yellow in pillows and decorative objects, plus fire and flame tones in a large rug bring the space to life.

Green has become an emblem for environmental awareness. It represents faith and immortality, is everlasting like mother nature, and, of course, is the color of the jungle, strong and reassuring.

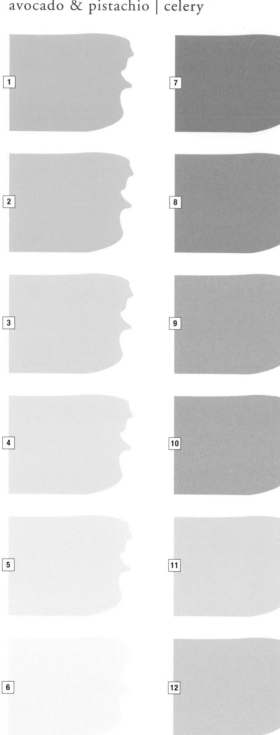

1 Springhill Green

2 Lime Twist

3 Mint Tea

4 Pine Sprigs

5 Chrome Green

6 Pale Pear

7 Gustavian Green

8 Spring Greens

9 Sage Green

10 Pine Tree

11 Mint Chocolate Chip

12 Chicory Tip

The green family is a happy and varied bunch of versatile shades, from palest celery to moody moss and olive through apple, mint, and verdant leaf tones.

ABOVE Julie Prisca's 19th-century coaching inn in northern France has a pale but pretty palette. Icy green rough plaster walls, a hint of lavender, and a good collection of jute and linen neutrals on upholstery help to create a soft coherence.

avocado & pistachio | apple

avocado & pistachio | olive

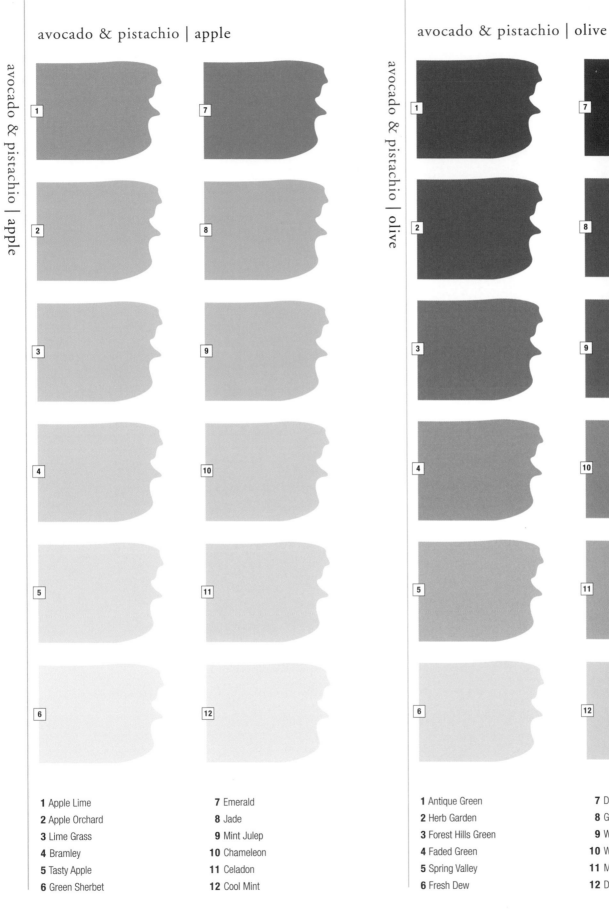

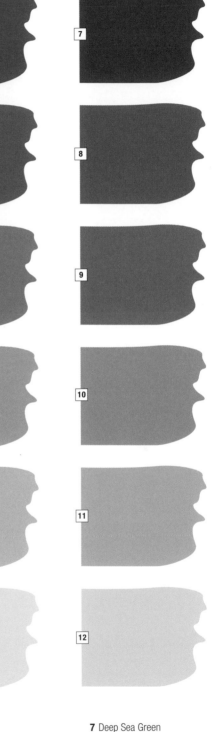

1 Apple Lime	**7** Emerald	**1** Antique Green	**7** Deep Sea Green
2 Apple Orchard	**8** Jade	**2** Herb Garden	**8** Gothic Green
3 Lime Grass	**9** Mint Julep	**3** Forest Hills Green	**9** Willow Grove
4 Bramley	**10** Chameleon	**4** Faded Green	**10** Winchester Sage
5 Tasty Apple	**11** Celadon	**5** Spring Valley	**11** Meadow
6 Green Sherbet	**12** Cool Mint	**6** Fresh Dew	**12** Dew

"Blue Hubbard 8053 by Martha Stewart Signature is a modern pale blue tint, slightly neutral. In the north light in my living room, it is a soft gray-blue, but in warm west light, with lots of windows, it almost takes on a celadon cast as it does in my sister's house in Connecticut. The green grass and trees outside reflect a pale celadon cast." ALEX BATES, WEST ELM

celery

At the delicate end of the green spectrum lie the leafy celery shades that are elegant, appealing, and sometimes barely there. From palest celadon to Gustavian gray-greens and historical shades such as Farrow & Ball's pale greens, these classically understated tones work across a number of surfaces, from woodwork to walls and architectural detailing. Especially popular in the northern hemisphere are the sage green shades that take their cue from historic houses. These classic shades never lose their appeal and have been revived by Fine Paints of Europe in the U.S. and Farrow & Ball on both sides of the Atlantic. Celery is always scrupulously smart for front doors as well as parlors, especially combined with racing green in a heritage combination, used on garden furniture and exterior woodwork as much as inside. These colorswork best in matte rather than glossy finishes.

Gray-greens remind us of the color of an olive leaf. These shades are usually not intense but soft, cool, and muted. They work well with creams, browns, and ochers, as well as royal blues and paler blues, especially when punctuated with deep browns and off-whites. Use slightly richer tones to combine with soft madder reds or pale rose for a classic complementary association that is fresh and uplifting. Such gentle associations work for guest rooms, living rooms, and Swedish-style dining rooms. They are at their best when combined with muted shades of toning colors.

THIS PAGE A floor-to-ceiling application of ethereal and calming soft mint allows abundant natural light to refract onto matte and gloss surfaces in a minimalist bedroom. It creates additional, dancing light in an empty but appealing space.

OPPOSITE Crisply feminine tones of palest celery and divine rosebud pink prove that using complementary shades on the color wheel do not always have to produce a dramatic contrast or be applied in violent hues.

forest symphony
In a palette that combines gray-greens and shades of gilt and faded wood, this antiques-led living room by Lynn von Kersting evokes a woodland story, with soft fern tones, the gold of fall leaves, and bracken.

gustavian green
In northern climates the muddied tones of Swedish greens and purposeful blues chosen by Peri Wolfman work well alongside wooden tones and a range of dirty whites, which absorb the light and enrich the atmosphere.

forest symphony | above

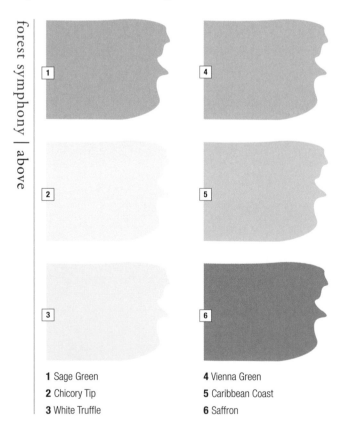

1 Sage Green
2 Chicory Tip
3 White Truffle
4 Vienna Green
5 Caribbean Coast
6 Saffron

gustavian green | above

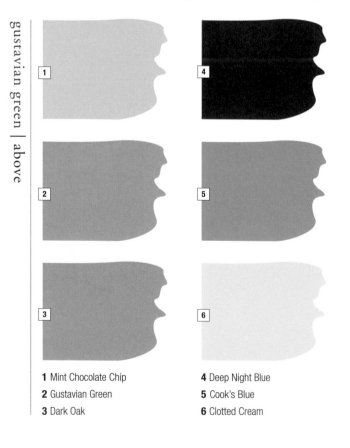

1 Mint Chocolate Chip
2 Gustavian Green
3 Dark Oak
4 Deep Night Blue
5 Cook's Blue
6 Clotted Cream

fried green tomatoes

Nature's palettes are always a source of inspiration. The delicious complementary shades of tomato red and apple orchard green refresh, revive, and bring a sense of permanent summer to a cheerful bedroom, where the outdoors is not far away.

1 Sage Green
2 Spring Greens
3 Pelican Gray
4 Mother of Pearl
5 Ruby Red
6 Full Bloom

OPPOSITE Snappy fresh
apple in a hallway gives instant
impact and a lively welcome.

THIS PAGE Muted apple
tones are a period classic, used
in milky paints in New England.

"Apple tones are hugely versatile greens. Both warm and subtle, they steer a course between garden green and muted olive. Farrow & Ball's Cooking Apple Green works marvellously well in combination with Pitch Blue and off-whites to give a fresh, warming feel to kitchens and dining areas." SARAH COLE, DIRECTOR, FARROW & BALL

apple

The true green of apples and the garden is at once clear and comforting. Perfect when combined with rich oak or pale ash and beech furniture, these tones provide a bright and reassuring backdrop given their associations with everything sustainable and wholesome. They work best when applied in a flat rather than glossy color and are perfect for bedrooms, kitchens, and dining areas or in spaces where concentration is required.

These apple greens, like lilacs, are capable of mutating throughout the day from pale apple to deep leaf green, so experiment with them on a piece of lining paper and observe the differing effects before committing to drenching a room in a color you may not be sure about. Apple shades work well with deep blues and bright whites as well as neutrals for a breezy, friendly palette, while complementary reds will provide sharp focus and more punch. They are quite strong tones in their own right and don't need too many distracting hues to accompany them, so keep the palette limited.

Exercise caution at the limey end of the scale. Sharp lime only really works on a small area as an accent in northern climates. It can look terrible in the cold light of the U.K. and northern Europe—not only too loud, but capable of draining the color from your face, too, as light bounces away from it. Be sure not to let colors become too acidic, as this will push them too far towards an unflattering, and therefore undesirable, yellow.

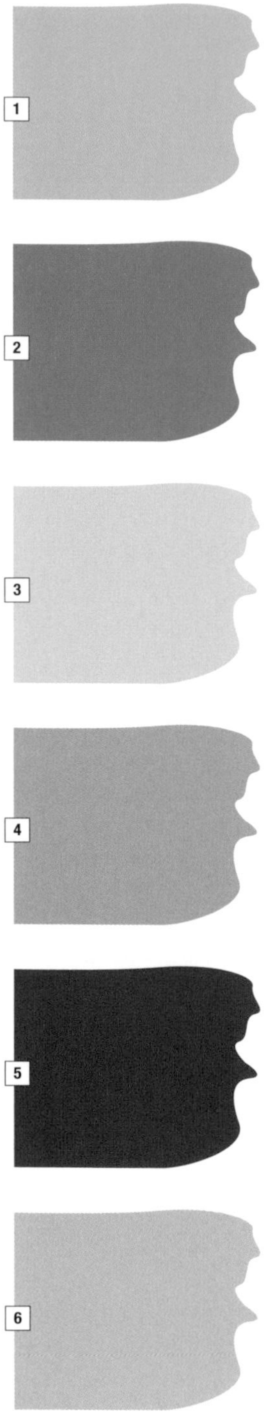

1 Mint Julep
2 Emerald
3 String
4 Dark Beige
5 Blazer Red
6 Fashion Pink

sage haven
Muted greens are the most successful of all for calming, comfortable living areas that are easy to spend time in. Teamed with creamery whites and rose pink reds they make a palette of soft complementary tones that are restful and not raucuous, and quite different from a rich tomato red and a vivid leaf green.

apple diner On the tasteful side of the acid green spectrum, this lively apple green is one that mutates considerably according to the time of day. In the morning or in gray light, it can appear quite pale, but faced with bright sunlight or the full force of daytime, it will take on richer, deeper tones.

1 Bramley
2 Midnight Green
3 Paddington Blue
4 Blue Bayou
5 Natural White
6 Seed Pod

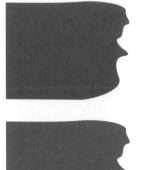

"From the enveloping earthy shade of an entire grove to the icon of a dry martini, olive is a soothing green, so natural in its ability to pose as a complement to many other hues. Thoughtful and reminiscent, its natural partners are rich browns, luscious plums, or enticing reds." JACKIE JORDAN, DIRECTOR OF COLOR MARKETING, SHERWIN-WILLIAMS

THIS PAGE The perfect pale olive, this gloriously subtle wall color combines the richness of green with the subtlety of gray to produce a warming but smart backdrop to rustic farmhouse walls and dark wood furniture and flooring.

OPPOSITE A combination of the forest tones of olive, moss and fern gives off peaceful, environmentally sound vibes in a child's room. Complementary reds provide accents, and shades of blue are a suprising but successful finishing touch.

olive

Cool khaki, mellow moss, and safari greens comprise the olive scale, in which the more somber but subtle greens reside. In color preference tests men often prefer these muted shades to other brighter greens. Warm but considered, they are a good choice for smart living and dining areas, maybe less suited to bedrooms, but can be reassuring in work areas. They have an ability to remain muted in the background while still making a subliminal color statement: versatile and enriching.

From almost taupe gray-greens to rich, deep moss via a brighter leaf green, this collection of shades is at the cooler end of the green spectrum. While green may be considered unlucky by some, it is a color whose time is right, with the emphasis on renewal and sustainability at the forefront of every designer's and decorator's agenda. Sludgy greens in particular, which are infinitely versatile, are popular with decorators.

Good team players with olive are the fall shades of faded gold and deep russet taken from the complementary side of things, while analogous shades that sit well with olive shades are cool taupes and browns, particularly the sandy beige and almost neutral tones, as well as yellow ocher through to pale lemon tones, and blues of any shade. Team them with shades of oatmeal and off-white rather than pure white, so that their subtlety is not stamped upon by too stark a contrast.

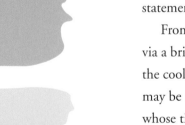

1 Faded Green
2 Pine Tree
3 Cornforth White
4 Beige Sand
5 Brassy Gold
6 London Burgundy

green mist In a David Collins' living room,
smart tones of gray-greens, faded olive, and deep bamboo conjure morning mist and intriguing hues of barely there greens to produce a rich but subtle palette that declares elegant comfort and is quite engrossing in its inspired selection of elusive shades.

chinese green Designer David Carter

uses aged and distressed bottle-green walls as a backdrop for an ancient Chinese sign, quirky tasselled floor lamps, and a vivid jade green table. These are deep, rich colors that definitely make a statement.

moroccan mix Designer Nathan

Turner's apartment is a Moroccan-inspired den where he combines ethnic-themed food with decoration in a palette of sharp gold tones with muted greens and rich reds against a backdrop of pearly off-white.

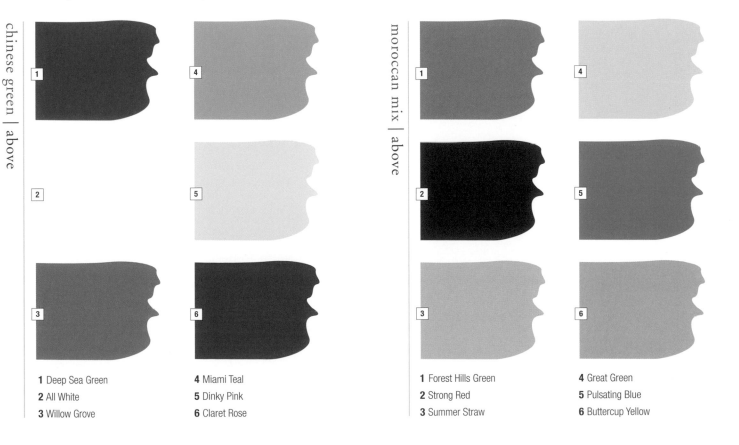

chinese green | above

moroccan mix | above

1 Deep Sea Green

2 All White

3 Willow Grove

4 Miami Teal

5 Dinky Pink

6 Claret Rose

1 Forest Hills Green

2 Strong Red

3 Summer Straw

4 Great Green

5 Pulsating Blue

6 Buttercup Yellow

earth
& clay

papaya
putty
nutmeg
acorn
beeswax
ocher
polished plaster
pueblo
dark oak
allspice
brown sugar
oxblood
acacia honey
red fox
ginger
red brick
savannah
walnut
tan
mustard
mink
cracked wheat
paprika
santa fe
mud flat
terra-cotta
tupelo taupe
sable fur
noisette
mocha
mahogany
bitter chocolate
wenge
iroko

ALL ABOUT BROWN

Brown earth tones are natural shades often associated with their areas of provenance—Mexican adobe, Moroccan Kasbah colors, Scandinavian barn red, or the coastal lime of west coast England. Never vivid or strong, the earth colors tend to be dark, gentle, and cozy in outlook, always keeping the peace and offering a reassuring haven, wherever they appear.

Earth colors are never crude. They remind us of the natural pigments from which they are derived, such as raw or burnt umber, and are as popular with artists as they are with decorators. Earth tones are colors we respond to naturally and their warm tones work well with any light in any location. Perfect decorating tools indeed.

Just as browns of all shades are popular with fashion designers, they also influence and inspire many interior decorators, both contemporary and historical. Designers Kelly Hoppen, Michael Reeves, and Jonathan Reed are all known for their use of luxurious tones of mole, beige, and subtle spicy shades when creating fine, inviting spaces that shout class and elegance. The Bloomsbury Set employed many shades of earth brown at their country retreat Charleston, in Sussex, England, while the Victorians were very fond of deep brown woodwork and earthy tones on fabrics and walls, as was William Morris, the arts and crafts designer. During the 1960s it seemed as though the earthy palettes containing rich shades of brown and orange were the only colors you could possibly consider decorating your home with, right down to mottled earthenware pottery for table settings and faded flame corduroy sofas being all the rage and seen everywhere.

Brown is the perfect diplomat—neither attention-seeking nor a shrinking violet, it is calm, steady and adaptable in any environment.

While brown was once considered ubiquitous and subsequently boring, it is in fact a deeply enriching color whose wholesale revival has endured many changes of fashion within the interiors world, purely because of its versatility and emotional baggage. Think of the comfortable associations with a steaming cup of hot chocolate, the richly varied gleaming and glossy tones of dark espresso, the creamy textured finish of fudge, or the fascinating patina of baked brownies.

Earth colors are timeless and organic their naturally warm tones working well with any light and in any location. Use them in chalky finishes for an enveloping sense of wellbeing.

Surface and finish are most important when it comes to the brown palette. Wood is of course a vital element in earth-inspired palettes, its natural textures and variations providing additional depth to any brown story. A wooden floor, panelled walls, or striking pieces of sold furniture are often used successfully as the main color in an earth-inspired palette, together with a variety of basketware for additional textural interest. Wood combines well with analogous shades of brick red, smoky minks, or cinnamon and cloves to complete the picture.

Key colors that also complement an earth palette include delicate shades of celery, celadon, or apple at the subtle side of things or sharp yellows, topaz, and burnt flame at the attention-grabbing end. The spicy tones of cinnamon and the more orange earth colors combine well with Mediterranean sky blue, just as the buildings of a medina blend effortlessly with summer skies in a knocked-back version of the classic blue and orange complementary partnership. An equally good relationship is that of vivid swimming pool blue teamed with the color of terra-cotta tiles.

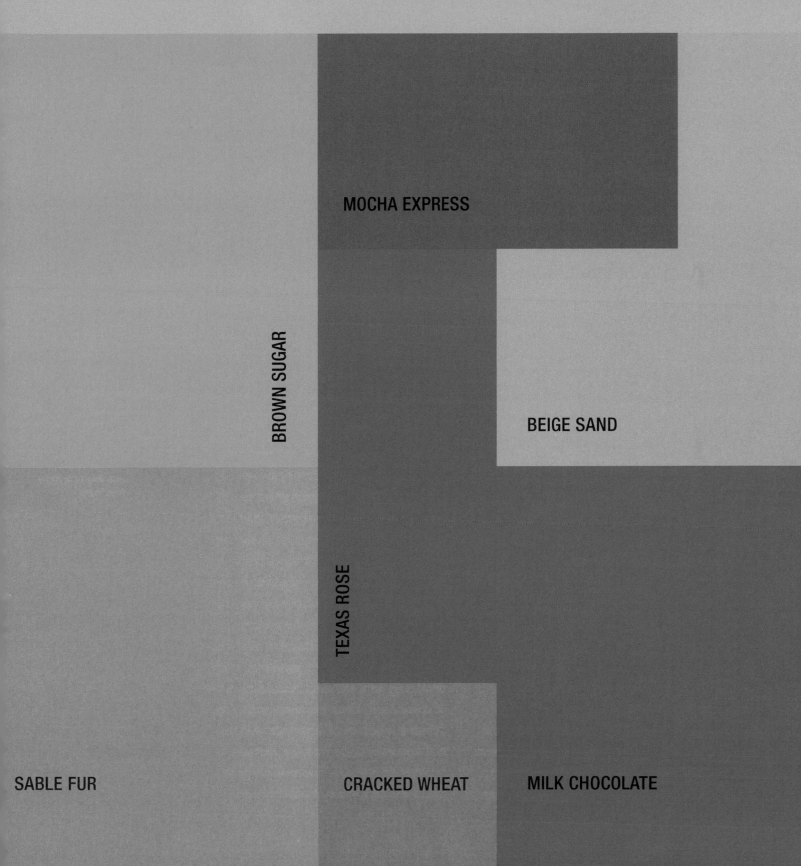

MUD FLAT

"When used on exteriors, earthy tones make a home look like it is part of its environment, while they can be used indoors to create a warm, open, and grounded atmosphere." ANNE ROSSELT, PLASCON PAINTS

MOCHA EXPRESS

BROWN SUGAR

BEIGE SAND

TEXAS ROSE

SABLE FUR

CRACKED WHEAT

MILK CHOCOLATE

Chocolate notes, spicy flavors, and the subtle tones of mole and adobe create happy combinations of earth colors that are scrupulously smart and richly defining.

USING BROWN Browns are perfect in spaces where warmth and comfort, simple luxury, and fine backdrops are required. The paler tones of mole and plaster are ideal in rooms where you wish to place an emphasis on art pictures or delicate fabrics such as self-patterned silks or damasks, floaty sheers, or nubbly textured fabrics such as linen, cord, or cotton damask.

Combining tone-on-tone beige, taupe, pale chocolate, and saffron, for instance, creates a wholesome story that is interesting but restful. These are tones that don't shout their presence, don't dominate the proceedings, but do provide an imperceptible sense of peace and proportion.

When working with these hues it is extremely important to use the right form of paint. Anything glossy or shiny will look unnatural and will reflect the light, making any space appear smaller. Instead, use textured or matte paint to make the color glow and add depth to the wall so it seems more natural and more spacious. Earthy palettes always work well on textured surfaces, so consider a rough plaster effect, either in physical form or by applying random layers of color to ape a broken surface.

Keeping the ceiling white when you are applying earth colors to the walls will allow light to bounce from it and not draw attention to it, thereby making the room look higher.

Francesca Wezel has painted her drawing room a beautiful dark brown, using a limewash as a base. The room is exposed to the southwest and benefits from a good deal of natural light. During sunset the room lights up like a dream, creating amazing tones that make you feel as though you are in a cozy, atmosphere that seems to hug and protect you without being too dark. The surface looks like soft velvet and gives off a sense of well-being. Such tones are beautiful and will never date.

The middle-range of browns, particularly shades of toffee or toast, can be warm or cool, depending on their tone, but are definitely calm, subtle shades to work with. Caramel and cinnamon stories are well-suited to creamy taupes and shades of oatmeal and pale butter.

In living rooms and bedrooms, strong brown schemes often work well. Although the use of deep brown is a statement in itself, it is also perfectly complemented by splashes of vivid or pale turquoise and pink for a bolder finish. Introduce these accent colors by means of rugs, artwork, china, and glass or pillows and throws.

Bathrooms, with their good supply of chrome surfaces, benefit from spots of brown in the form of pinky terra-cotta walls that provide warmth and flatter skin tones under artificial and natural light, while organic shades on walls, tiles, and floors are enduringly popular.

At the richer end of the spectrum, definite browns are a natural choice for architectural detailing such as doors, paneling, dados, coving, cornicing, and skirting. According to the strength of color used, these elements will either clearly define a space, or, if kept pale and interesting, will become subtle framing elements. Rich browns on wooden floors or on paneling never fail to evoke a sense of solidity and warmth.

OPPOSITE TOP LEFT In the hallway of a period house toffee and ocher tones combine in the patterned wallpaper, with glimpses of colorwashed walls in a study beyond.

OPPOSITE TOP RIGHT This Moroccan retreat designed by Studio KO architects of Paris is deliciously warmed by stonewashed tones applied directly to plaster walls.

OPPOSITE BOTTOM LEFT A faux suede bedhead in smart mole tones provides pleasing punctuation in a bedroom where dark wood and wheaten beige complete a subtle earthy palette.

OPPOSITE BOTTOM RIGHT A rich mix of linen, chenille, fur, and velvet fabrics in mocha and chocolate shades sit perfectly against a wall painted in flat, chalky mud tones in this living room designed by Bernie de Le Cuona.

earth & clay | cinnamon

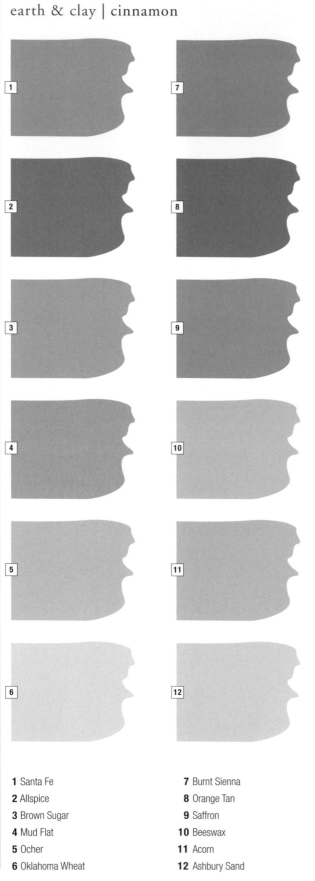

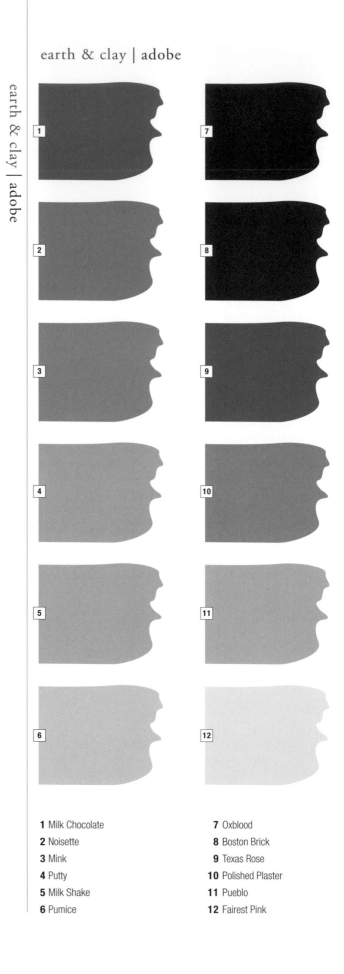

1 Santa Fe	**7** Burnt Sienna	**1** Milk Chocolate	**7** Oxblood
2 Allspice	**8** Orange Tan	**2** Noisette	**8** Boston Brick
3 Brown Sugar	**9** Saffron	**3** Mink	**9** Texas Rose
4 Mud Flat	**10** Beeswax	**4** Putty	**10** Polished Plaster
5 Ocher	**11** Acorn	**5** Milk Shake	**11** Pueblo
6 Oklahoma Wheat	**12** Ashbury Sand	**6** Pumice	**12** Fairest Pink

earth & clay | chocolate

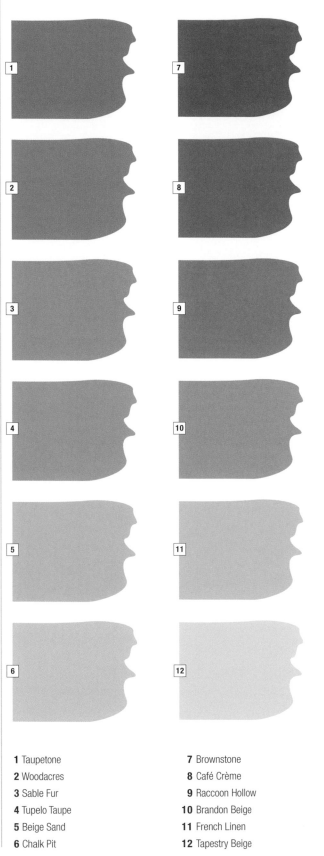

1 Taupetone	**7** Brownstone	**1** Cup O'Java	**7** Mahogany
2 Woodacres	**8** Café Crème	**2** Saddle Brown	**8** Mocha Express
3 Sable Fur	**9** Raccoon Hollow	**3** Savannah	**9** Truffle
4 Tupelo Taupe	**10** Brandon Beige	**4** Bitter Chocolate	**10** Cracked Wheat
5 Beige Sand	**11** French Linen	**5** Dark Oak	**11** Smooth Pebble
6 Chalk Pit	**12** Tapestry Beige	**6** Nutmeg	**12** Camel's Back

THIS PAGE Vibrant hot spice walls are defined and heightened by deep chocolate woodwork and detailing. Complementary blue accents in the form of small cups on the table may be small scale, but provide a jolt that makes the colors sing in this enriching, traditional dining space.

OPPOSITE Jamie Drake's masterful command of color combines golden cinnamon tones in painted patchwork on the walls with soft turquoise green at the window in his New York apartment. Tonal variations on the spice theme create an enveloping sense of warmth.

"Cinnamon tones have a wonderful rich quality. The burnt-orange undertone creates a warm, sociable, creative, and friendly environment, perfect for a kitchen, dining room, or living room. Cinnamon tones also look wonderful with wood, adding to the cozy ambiance." ANNE ROSSELT, PLASCON PAINTS

cinnamon

Colorful cinnamon tones are perfectly suited to rooms with northern or cool light, such as the East Coast U.S. or northern Europe; as a collection of earth-toned colors warmed by yellow ocher, these warming colors work in all light levels. They instantly warm and embrace the space to make even the dingiest bedroom or living area come alive. Use cinnamon in varying tones such as saffron, brown sugar, and nutmeg for a cohesive and interesting harmonious story. Add in a glossy sheen or additional texture on decorative accessories in the form of velvet pillows, silk throws, or faux suede upholstery for maximum effect, and tone it down with deep shades of chocolate and ebony. Or contrast it with complementary muddy greens for a totally integrated palette that is rich and cozy.

Vibrant, spicy earth tones are traditionally associated with the locations where they are most often found. In particular they are found working their flavorsome magic in stunning exotic locations such as Morocco, Tuscany, and Africa, where the sunny climate and generous natural light teases tonal treats from paintwork. In the desert of Arizona or the pueblos of New Mexico, the delicious spicy hues of ginger, cumin, and nutmeg create a richness that is grounding yet rich and bright. But don't be afraid to use this palette in less exotic situations as the hot, warm tones will still work, especially when teamed with other warm colors.

1 Brown Sugar
2 Beige Sand
3 Golden Yellow
4 Mandarin Fruit
5 Gray Suede
6 Leather

island spice
New York designer Clodagh has put together natural clove-colored logs, soft washes of ocher on the walls, and a rich mix of spice tones on fabrics, flooring, and furnishings that team with wall-mounted artwork for a superb exercise in using analogous shades, from pale tangerine to cinnamon and saffron.

feeling the heat
In a Moroccan-inspired bedroom, deep chocolate browns anchor a scheme that relies on orange ocher walls and accents of russet for its color. Sometimes subtle color accents can provide a strong sense of color in a room.

bathed in spice
Fabulously rich, red colorwashed walls allow light to dance around a rustic bathroom in this Irish cottage. A lead bath bought from a Paris flea market provides more broken color in a space that is dark but interesting.

feeling the heat | above

1	4
2	5
3	6

1 Acorn   **4** Red Rock
2 Orange Tan   **5** Chili Pepper
3 Clover White   **6** Jet Night

bathed in spice | above

1	4
2	5
3	6

1 Texas Rose   **4** Meadowlands Green
2 Tapestry Beige   **5** Racing Green
3 Cotton Ball   **6** Olympus Green

THIS PAGE Simply brimming with broken color, these luscious toffee-toned walls conjure the warmth of adobe and the subtlety of a colorwash in a space that could lean towards the clinical were it not for these many interesting layers of texture.

OPPOSITE The adobe walls do the color talking here. Fantastic painterly tones are a result of the earth, plaster, and straw walls, designed to counteract the fierce Moroccan heat of this Corbusier-like house, designed by Studio KO architects, Karl Fournier and Olivier Marty.

"These colors are never crude. They remind you of the earth, of the pigments from which they came. They are grounded, stable, and secure and you can feel the relationship with their environment. Earthy tones are colors we respond to naturally and warmly. These colors work well with any light and in any location." FRANCESCA WEZEL, FRANCESCA'S PAINTS

adobe

Adobe walls are found in the same places where the sun beats strongly, such as southwestern U.S. and Africa, from Morocco to Yemen. The natural elements used in the formation of these thick, sometimes curved and uneven walls—earth, straw, clay, and plaster among them—often perform the dual role of absorbing the heat of the sun during the day and radiating it away from the house during the night, to make sleeping more comfortable.

Materials used in adobe walls often influence the color and style of the interior. Think of a Santa Fe pueblo building and its white, curved Mexican-style fireplace, which is both a focal point and an organic shape that may be echoed elsewhere in curved pieces of furniture. Adobe walls can be painted chalky white to help refract heat, but often their natural earthy hues are simply left to weather or are varnished to give the impression of a colorwashed wall with interesting layers of broken color forming on the uneven texture. Classic adobe colors include red iron oxide, clay and straw, faded plaster pink, and tones of mottled taupe. Studio KO architects, in their modern interpretation of adobe techniques, have created a fireplace in Marrakesh that dispenses with the curved organic form. It is clad in metal, follows the clean lines of contemporary design, and combines richly textured natural walls with a floor of painted, varnished concrete. The adobe-style walls and an earthbound palette create warmth.

treetop cool
South African architect Johann Slee's forest "treehouse" blurs the boundary of indoors and out. The interior space projects nature's palette back outdoors by means of complementary shades of leaf green and berry red. Enriching earth tones of rough plaster walls recreate the color story found in the surrounding forest.

mud, glorious mud

A symphony of browns is made interesting by combining plaster walls, a distressed leather headboard and a footboard on the bed, and a glossy sheen on the polished woodwork. Punctuated with white bedlinen and cherry wood bedside tables with brass fittings, who said brown is boring?

1 Milk Chocolate
2 Pumice
3 All White
4 Hadley Red
5 Monticello Rose
6 Toasted Bean

"By layering varying tones, mole adds real depth to a room. Add textures, then the room really becomes alive: reflective steel, metallic fabrics, glass, and lacquered surfaces add visual interest. Accent colors add a jolt and careful lighting should complement the color tones, without detracting from the calm, tranquil feeling the color mole emits." MICHAEL REEVES

THIS PAGE A soothing mix of red brick, aged oak, and elephant gray set off with a cool beige seat pillow is a sublime combination of subtle colors that are sympathetic and restful.

OPPOSITE Fabulously chic yet comfortable, these deep mole walls change shade by night, especially when lit by grandiose chandeliers formed from multiple empty bottles Designer Virginia Fisher provides texture in the form of sisal matting, and elegant accents appear as artwork and on the upholstered dining chairs.

mole

The mole shades are the tasteful taupes of the earth palette, the chic and sophisticated neutral-leaning shades that encompass the red-tinged browns of camel and mushroom, together with the soft, textural beauty of suede and linen, faux fur, and leather.

Mole can be sharp and sophisticated when used as a palette of toning shades. Rich, subtle, and astoundingly elegant, these shades work well when displaying their natural affinity with the other stronger earth colors, as part of a palette that combines shades such as spice and saffron, red brick, and mocha teamed with neutrals such as gray, toasted oats, or latte. Mole shades may also shine when defined and rendered smart by black detailing or accented with suggestions of the warm reds that form part of their base color.

Straddling the boundary of earth tones, the night and day shades, and even straying into the panna cotta and cappuccino hues, what keeps these colors firmly down to earth is their inherent cool brown nature. They work beautifully when emphasized with unusual accents such as flame, burnt ginger, Chinese reds, or sharp lime greens. Natural colors such as vanilla and clotted cream work well with this palette, as do natural textures such as limestone, linen, glass, and granite. Warm, welcoming and a provider of reassuring tones, mole can be wonderfully utilized in rooms such as living areas and bedrooms where comfort is key.

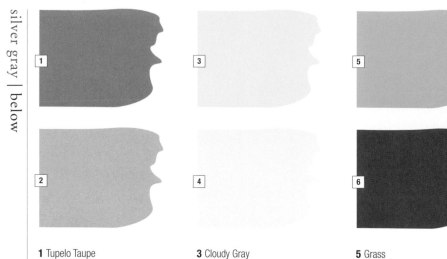

silver gray
Multiple metallic surfaces combine with the clear clay walls to make a sophisticated color statement, punctuated with black and white. Accents of green provided by foliage and flowers make a neat counterpoint to the neutral tones used elsewhere in the space on the walls, floor, and the furnishing fabrics.

1 Tupelo Taupe
2 Shadow Gray
3 Cloudy Gray
4 Cotton Ball
5 Grass
6 Jungle

1	
2	
3	
4	
5	
6	

fired earth The color brown is formed from

a mix of black and red in varying proportions, which is why brown
and red and black and red make such excellent color companions.
This palette of reds, orange-browns, and deep taupe walls is an
interesting and lively interpretation of a brown story.

1 Sable Fur
2 Flax
3 Savory Cream
4 Pumpkin Spice
5 Shy Cherry
6 Misty Morning

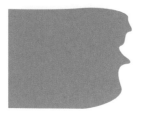

"Benjamin Moore's Bittersweet Chocolate 2114-10 is the perfect rich shade: neither too red or green. I tried a wide range to get this just-right shade. I painted my dining room in a satin finish with high-gloss creamy white trim. Paintings and blue and white china literally pop off of it." ALEX BATES, WEST ELM

THIS PAGE Designer Bernie de Le Cuona includes a fluid flash of analogous orange for a subtle take on the classic red and brown combination. Russet, cherrywood, jute, and cocoa all add to the delicious mix.

OPPOSITE Chocolate walls, the bedframe, and bedside furniture are the perfect counterpoint to white walls and drapes, softened with an indigo blue duvet, in this smart and sophisticated bedroom designed by Ilaria Miani.

chocolate

Chocolate is a hip and happening palette, since it made a dramatic comeback a decade ago as a serious color to use in the home. Hot chocolate is the color of dark wood and delicious treats, sleek and sophisticated, capable of appearing smart and contemporary, or creating a traditional polished effect. Or think of the toffee and caramel tones of animal fur, where tone-on-tone chocolate, butterscotch, and licorice combine in a mellifluous brown haze to denote soft comfort. From the rich, smooth and glossy bittersweet tones of deepest ebony to the chalky matte and opaque finish of limed oak, or the cocoa dust hues of chocolate truffles, chocolate-colored walls or floors may be treated so as to be reflective and

refined or dirtied up, to create a more informal appearance. Matte and chalky paints give depth to a room and make it look bigger, so in a small space, experiment with types of paints such as these for an enlarging effect.

Floors are the place where chocolate tones never fail to anchor a color scheme and provide dark definition. When used on walls, too, the deeply dark ambiance that emerges benefits from accent colors to brighten the effect. Vivid turquoise, lemon sherbet, and baby blue provide exciting tonal variations to lift such a scheme and prevent an overly masculine feel. Chocolate colors are formed by a mix of red and black, so it's no surprise that red with chocolate is a comfortable choice.

1 Mahogany
2 Salsa
3 Café Latte
4 Glimmer
5 Citronee
6 Seaport Blue

topaz & toffee
Jewel-bright accents on pillows, flowers, and accessories bring vivid life to this living room by designer Philip Gorrivan. The whole color balance in a room can be shifted by adding or subtracting bright pillows, pictures, and mirrors to or from a space. Topaz and turquoise are especially good foils for dark colors.

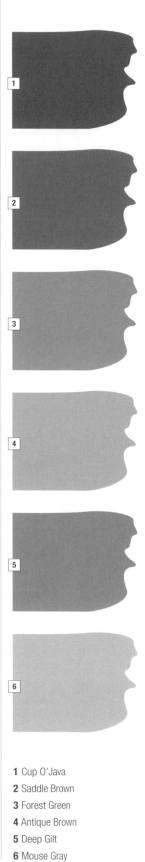

mocha living
Texture is important here in this tone-on-tone amalgamation of polished oak and linen, with alternate walls lined with cherry paneling and painted in bitter chocolate by 20th-century architect Patrick Gwynne. A symphony of browns, from the orange end of the spectrum to the rich and moody chocolate, predominate.

1 Cup O'Java
2 Saddle Brown
3 Forest Green
4 Antique Brown
5 Deep Gilt
6 Mouse Gray

night
& day

titanium white
chanel chic
nautical white
egyptian cotton
arctic fox
tundra ice
mother of pearl
polar bear
china cup
chalk
ice blue
silver birch
stainless steel
silver
chrome
gunmetal
pearl
gustavian gray
black truffle
jet
blackcurrant jelly
licorice
aniline black
carbon
black ash
blackboard
dove
gray ash
elephant gray
night sky
squid ink
pewter
charcoal
graphite

ALL ABOUT MONOCHROME

The monochrome tones are indispensable decorating tools, whether creating a simple black and white room or using them to define, punctuate, or neutralize a color scheme. The jury is out over whether black is a color, since an object will look black when all the wavelengths of the light spectrum are absorbed in its surface. Strictly speaking, black and white perform like light reflectors and absorbers, rather than containing particular pigments or being borne out of two or more other definite colors.

It is easy to dismiss black and white as an "easy" palette to work with, or even a predictable one. In fact it is a classic complementary partnership: graphic, clean, scrupulously elegant, and capable of being at once bold and understated. Think of the classic Chanel graphics and the couture clothes, cowhide, zebra stripes, the endless possibilities of black type on white paper. All of them are perfectly chic and astoundingly smart.

Black is a smart definer and surprisingly unobtrusive as an accent color when it appears on architectural details such as paneling, countertops, slate fireplaces, floors, and ceiling beams. Blacks tinted with blue provide a more reflective surface, while those at the gray end of the spectrum have a smoky tint that is seldom less than chic.

Pure white can be incredibly cold and gray if used in the wrong tones. The ice whites or pure whites will always need to be warmed by other richer shades or else they will bathe a room in a dull cast. But white as a decorating color choice encourages a clear mind, de-clutters the senses, and allows creative thought free rein. It provides a pure backdrop that enables us to create fresh and inviting spaces.

Gray, the median interloper between black and white, is chic and elegant. It is one of my favorite shades and I am fascinated by its endless versatility. Certainly not dull and boring, its crisp clean tones are capable of harnessing the best light from many other colors, throwing them all into perfect balance. Be inspired by the soft metallic sheen of an Armani suit or brushed steel, and how light bounces effortlessly off such surfaces to give a pleasing sheen. Gray is the perfect mixer, flattering all the other colors and allowing them to shine and be at their best.

Within this supposedly predictable palette are many other nuances on this far-from-narrow spectrum. The fragile alabaster shades, the glamorous metallic shades of silver, and the smoky slate tones that graduate towards midnight tones: deep, reflective anthracite, and, eventually, black.

Black, white, and gray are the "colorless" shades that are cool, smart, and endlessly adaptable. They work best in chic bedrooms, classic living areas, and contemporary kitchens.

Some rooms, where the color balance leans more toward black as the dominant color, are considered urban masculine spaces. This look is particularly associated with large bedrooms or kitchens where you find a lot of stainless steel hardware. To add a little femininity to such spaces, treat black in a room the same way as you would a little black dress and accessorize to your heart's content. Silver, reds, greens, and yellows, whether in vivid primary tones or knocked-back shades, all work with the dark neutral tones of black. In rooms where black is an important element in the color palette, it will look more striking when used in chalky matte tones on the walls. On furniture, black looks at its best when applied in a glossy finish, for a look that is sleek and sophisticated.

Black is a powerful shade, and too much of it can be uncomfortable to live with, bathing the room in dark mystery rather than a dramatic cast, so keep its importance in proportion.

"Monochromatic is the easiest scheme to achieve as it is based on one color, which is adjusted by adding white to lighten or black to darken, producing a tint or shade respectively." DAVID OLIVER, THE PAINT LIBRARY

STAINLESS STEEL

PEWTER

BLACKBOARD

SNOW WHITE

WHITE ICE

AIRFORCE BLUE

Black is a color with a permanent backstage pass when it comes to room design. Always there in the wings, not stealing the limelight, but an indispensable part of any successful color palette.

USING MONOCHROME Rooms that are predominantly decorated in white, gray, or black all benefit from accent colors, rich textures, or tone-on-tone layers of these shades to really bring them alive and provide an alternative color focus. For accent colors, choose from deep coral reds, faded lime greens, sharp turquoise, or bitter yellows for jolts of bright shades that are strong but not overpowering.

Stacked logs against white walls in a living room or dining space lend a warming texture to black and white spaces and hint at a Danish modern style, ever popular for urban apartments and contemporary country spaces. The whites in these rooms should be chosen with care, so as not to make any black tones act as a strong coolant in the space. If you use whites with a small amount of red or yellow ocher in them this will warm them through.

The mid-tone grays of flannel, pewter, and seal is created when gray is pushed towards the brown end of the spectrum. This whole brownish-gray spectrum mixes really well with harmonious earth colors such as bone, mushroom, and all shades of brown. Layer these colors tone on tone for a cohesive palette that lends itself to any room of the house, but is particularly restful for living rooms and bedrooms.

Mid-tone grays work wonderfully well on woodwork and are often surprising in their smartness. Although often dismissed as cold or dull, they are superb in combination with other monochrome shades, especially when teamed with cool white furniture and smart steely grays.

Texture, in the form of fabrics such as checked or striped gray-toned tweeds, felted wool, or woven linens, always adds depth to a plain scheme. For a warm gray, choose one that incorporates a dash of beige to take away chilly tones.

Gray as a color is capable of looking both stylish and completely cozy, from contemporary urban settings to informal rural retreats. It is a shade that is versatile and underrated. Use it as a warm, mellow evening color, or as a crisp daytime definer. Set it to work on walls or woodwork and enjoy its smart tones as a key part of a palette rather than as a throwaway accent.

Rich, dark grays, the color of anthracite and slate, are enriching tones that go with everything. They are especially good winter warming colors that complement white. Such a combination will give you a smart palette that is chic and urban in style. Be sure to apply wall color in a matte finish, then add layers of gloss or sheen by means of mirrors, crystal, or glass. Or paint wooden furniture in gloss tones for a sense of luxury.

Use black for defining details: as an edging on picture frames, piping on furniture, and punctuation around windows and on doors in the form of curtain poles and door furniture. When it does take center stage it provides deep drama, especially when mixed with reflective surfaces such as mirror and steel.

The classic black and white story is always at home in a bathroom, where clean white walls team well with black and white tiles on walls and floors. The same can be said for a kitchen, where this palette evokes the feel of a retro fifties diner.

OPPOSITE TOP LEFT Tone-on-tone snow whites are always sleek, even in northern light such as in this Belgian house designed by architect Axel Vervoordt.

OPPOSITE TOP RIGHT A gray-painted, Provençal-style period console table makes a delicious accent against soft white walls and a bleached and aged wooden floor.

OPPOSITE BOTTOM LEFT A warm-toned wooden floor will always soften any coldness in a space where cool whites and black accents would otherwise tend to dominate.

OPPOSITE BOTTOM RIGHT Gray is seriously smart and sophisticated when combined with crisp whites and defining black.

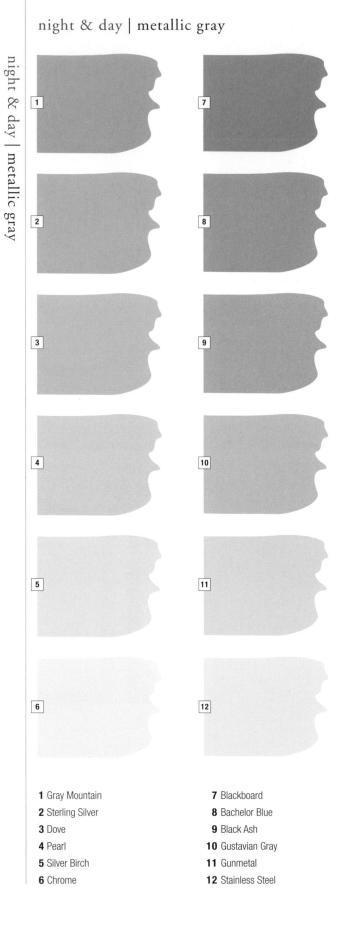

1 Nautical White	7 White Ice
2 Arctic Fox	8 Polar Bear
3 China Cup	9 Tundra Ice
4 Egyptian Cotton	10 Winter Snow
5 Chalk	11 Titanium White
6 Mother of Pearl	12 Snow White

1 Gray Mountain	7 Blackboard
2 Sterling Silver	8 Bachelor Blue
3 Dove	9 Black Ash
4 Pearl	10 Gustavian Gray
5 Silver Birch	11 Gunmetal
6 Chrome	12 Stainless Steel

The monochrome shades of black, white, and gray may lack strong color, but the contrast certainly packs a dramatic punch, whether used over large areas or as detailing in a space—perfect partners without being sleepy.

BELOW Ebony detailing on an ironwork bedframe and curtain pole, in addition to dark brown basketware and mahogany chairs, provides crisp definition in an otherwise soft white bedroom.

1 Charcoal
2 Deep Slate
3 Graphite
4 Elephant Gray
5 Pewter
6 Pelican Gray

7 Squid Ink
8 Airforce Blue
9 Bluff Cove
10 Silver Mink
11 Ice Blue
12 Gray Ash

"My perfect white, Fine Paints of Europe 0001, is not too cold or warm. I painted the walls, ceiling, and floors of my beach house in high gloss. The light pours in and bounces all around. It is particularly dramatic at dusk; it filters through the blinds and casts painterly shadows across the living room floor. The quality and depth of this traditional Dutch-style paint can't be beaten." ALEX BATES, WEST ELM

snow

Titanium white is perhaps the perfect snow color. Pure white is mixed with a touch of black to produce an almost imperceptible gray tinge that produces a pure, slightly cool white. Such a cool color needs to be warmed by other colors for it to succeed in a color palette. Combine it with rich reds, brownish greens (rather than yellow-greens, which will make it seem even colder), and regal blues for a crisp nautical edge. Soften it with slate gray felted wool throws, wood-framed furniture or a selection of interesting black and white accessories such as framed photographs, steel-based lamps, or curtain poles.

Pure white walls can be stylish but need careful handling. Brilliant white can turn out to be just as difficult to work with as yellow, so be prepared to introduce warm and enriching colors to accompany it, especially in an already gray northern light. Whereas brilliant white walls in a Greek island retreat will sing with cheer, they will actually throw a gray cast in a Washington loft or New York brownstone. The trick is in the mix and ensuring the right level of purity. When it is right, pure white is invigorating and refreshing. Try incorporating a variety of whites for a warmer finish. Stick to a warm white on the ceiling and cooler whites on woodwork and detailing. Many designers revel in all-white living spaces, as they provide a blank canvas in which they can consider other concepts without too much visual distraction.

THIS PAGE This is a glorious example of the pure beauty that a monochrome palette is capable of producing. It is all about using the right combination of warm whites, slate, and midnight black, accented with oatmeal, pale gray, and splashes of texture.

OPPOSITE Bluff white shutters and walls provide a serene backdrop in a living room, where red and white ticking pillows are a crisp counterpoint.

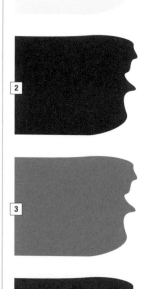

1 Jute
2 Charcoal
3 Forest Hills Green
4 Turkish Coffee
5 Bronzed Brown
6 Walled Garden

lofty whites Vicente Wolf designs New York

lofts like no one else. This impeccably sophisticated space combines simple styling and intriguing amounts of forest and khaki shades set against brown and taupe fabrics. The antique gray walls and ceiling and limestone-tiled floor form an unobtrusive backdrop that allows the furniture to speak.

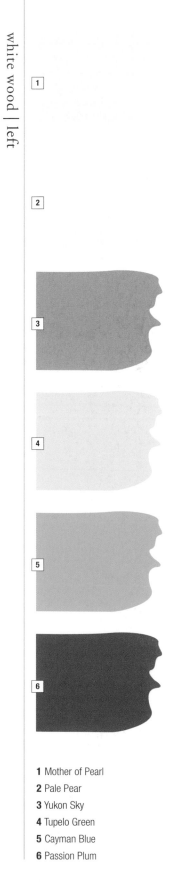

white wood

In an all-white room it is important to vary the whites and introduce splashes of color to break up the space. Jolts of lilac and turquoise counterpoint the sage green and white checkerboard floor in this bright and breezy dining area. A combination of whites is a clean and uplifting palette, as long as you choose carefully.

1 Mother of Pearl
2 Pale Pear
3 Yukon Sky
4 Tupelo Green
5 Cayman Blue
6 Passion Plum

"Metallic finishes will reflect light and bring life to matte surfaces. I love creating layers of interesting textures and often use steely dark grays and jet black mixed with delicate, dirty off-whites to create smart, flattering spaces." DOMINIQUE KIEFFER

metallic gray

The shimmering tones of metallic finishes such as silver, bronze, crystal, steel, and glass have graduated from interesting adjuncts to center stage in many contemporary color schemes. Rich, interesting tones are being created by many designers, including Michael Reeves and Kelly Hoppen, with a sensitive use of gloss that, used in the right proportion and on the right surfaces, provides glamour rather than glitz, taste rather than tack.

The neutral elegance of metallic tones provides a glow that enhances classic palettes such as the gray, weathered look of Scandinavian interiors or more traditional French country schemes. At the contemporary cutting edge, silvery walls provide a sharp backdrop for oversized mirrors, statement-making crystal chandeliers, and satin fabrics. From the pearl gray shades of zinc to pale silver leaf, sophisticated gray tones look amazing on woodwork and also work as definition on furniture, picture frames, and mirrors. Metallic gray and steel work well hand-in-hand with indigo or slightly knocked-back fuchsia accents for a smart and understated color story.

To make sure gray tones are warm, add a dash of beige to remove any lingering cool tones. Pearl gray is a good, mellow evening color and is capable of working well in urban or country settings. Used on floors, reflective glossy grays make a perfect lively anchor for a combination of monochrome tones.

deco shimmer

The combination of reflective surfaces and very appealing colorwashed and glazed walls, mixed with white-painted period paneling and touches of deep claret, produce a smart, updated 1930s color palette.

deco shimmer | opposite

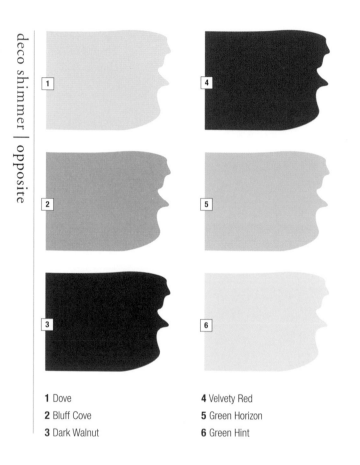

1 Dove
2 Bluff Cove
3 Dark Walnut

4 Velvety Red
5 Green Horizon
6 Green Hint

pewter perfection

A gray symphony of pewter-toned woodwork and walls treated with a glaze of metallic paint echoes traditional Swedish style, with painted furniture featuring colors that are cool enough to mimic an ice house, yet also retain an element of warmth and welcome.

pewter perfection | above

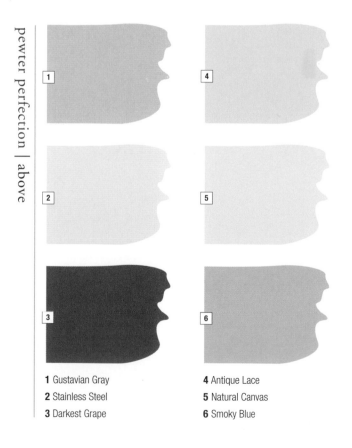

1 Gustavian Gray
2 Stainless Steel
3 Darkest Grape

4 Antique Lace
5 Natural Canvas
6 Smoky Blue

Reflective surfaces add a fascinating dimension to the metallic colors of gunmetal, steel, and cozy gray. Combine metallic paint with glossy furniture for the most vivid effect.

> "Combining black with white may not seem an obvious pairing, but it throws up smart, chic solutions when placed alongside harmonious shades of white and gray and punctuated with shots of color. I love the clarity produced by these sharp, clear tones." JOHN BARMAN

THIS PAGE At the charcoal end of the gray spectrum, these painted stair risers and baseboards give graphic definition to a curved staircase, creating an architectural statement in a tall hallway.

OPPOSITE A graphite-inspired bedroom mixes a masculine palette with chrome styling and a contemporary colorful wall panel by Kelly Stuart Graham.

slate

Although dark, moody grays and near-blacks are colors that are perhaps more associated with incidental elements in a palette—used on painted floors, as detailing on picture frames, and furniture edging—they are in fact quite stunning used as a main color in a room too. Combine them with white, rich woody tones and paler grays or steely blues and ocher for a sleek, smart palette that works in a number of settings, from cool, urban retro chic to classic, pared-down country or traditional interiors.

Midnight black and blue are powerful tones and are best softened with shots of other colors, while slate grays are perfect with whites for schemes that are reminiscent of felted wool blankets and linen sheets.

Slate floors are particularly successful paired with creams and sage greens or used as foils for black architectural features in a room with paler neutrals. Other colors that harmonize well with a deep grayish black story include oxblood, celadon, moody gray-blues, and a richer Shaker blue. Keep any blues and greens muted rather than bright for the most sophisticated combinations, and use the citric shades of lemon and lime, or fuchsia and orange, for a more complementary approach. Tone-on-tone combinations are best approached by using elements of all the night and day shades. Use metallic surfaces in the form of chandeliers, mirrors, or chrome-edged furniture with luxurious velvet or satin throws in delicious grays, and indulge in jet woodwork.

tropical glamour
An edgy mauve on a rough concrete wall is perfectly counterpointed with ebony gloss floorboards, deep gray woodwork, a black metal bedframe, and a gray-tiled sunken bathtub in a palette that is ultra smart for a bedroom.

black notes
Frank Faulkner's superb conglomeration of a high-gloss white floor, ice gray walls, and several black accents in the form of furniture and accessories is a classical, and very successful, interpretation of the monochrome theme.

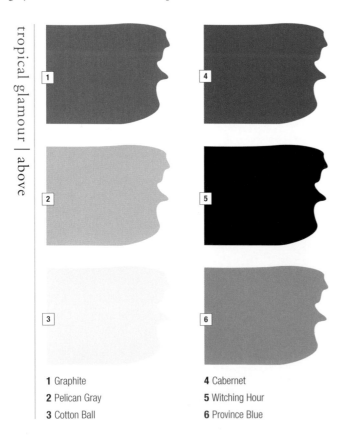

tropical glamour | above

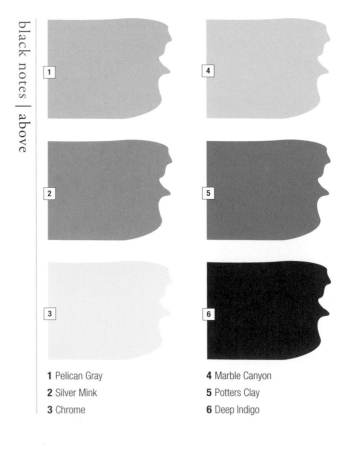

black notes | above

1 Graphite
2 Pelican Gray
3 Cotton Ball
4 Cabernet
5 Witching Hour
6 Province Blue

1 Pelican Gray
2 Silver Mink
3 Chrome
4 Marble Canyon
5 Potters Clay
6 Deep Indigo

fine dining
Midnight oil-tinted walls are framed by designer Alexandra Champalimaud with flat-painted crown molding and built-in cabinetry, inset with marbled paneling and baseboards. They make a rich and textured counterpoint to the leather-bound dining chairs and glossy wood on the table and the floor.

1 Charcoal
2 Lantern Light
3 Clotted Cream
4 Newburg Green
5 Hollow Brown
6 Sag Harbor Gray

northern lights
Black-painted kitchen cabinets are the only dark shades against white walls and eaves in Peri Wolfman's country kitchen. An aged butcher's table and a stripped floor provide an element of warmth in the monochrome space.

entirely tar
In Normandy, Dominique Kieffer's utility room combines deep gray, tar, and white for a serious-looking practical space. The draped linen conceals white appliances while clean linen is stored in a seed chest painted elephant gray.

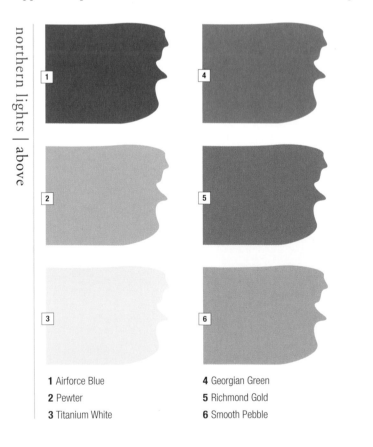

northern lights | above

1 Airforce Blue
2 Pewter
3 Titanium White
4 Georgian Green
5 Richmond Gold
6 Smooth Pebble

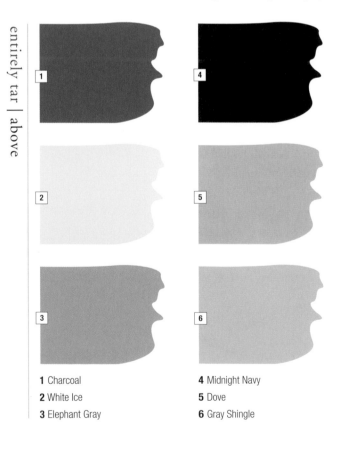

entirely tar | above

1 Charcoal
2 White Ice
3 Elephant Gray
4 Midnight Navy
5 Dove
6 Gray Shingle

green & black Kristiina Ratia

uses greenery to accent and enliven clean monochromes in a screened outdoor room where natural light is in abundance. Plants bring the outside in as well as help refresh the pale scheme.

safari plains Gentle olive and beige tones

on walls and floor are neatly framed by designer Jeffrey Bilhuber with clean white woodwork. An oversized paneled door painted in deep elephant gray makes a majestic statement, counterpointed by the chairs.

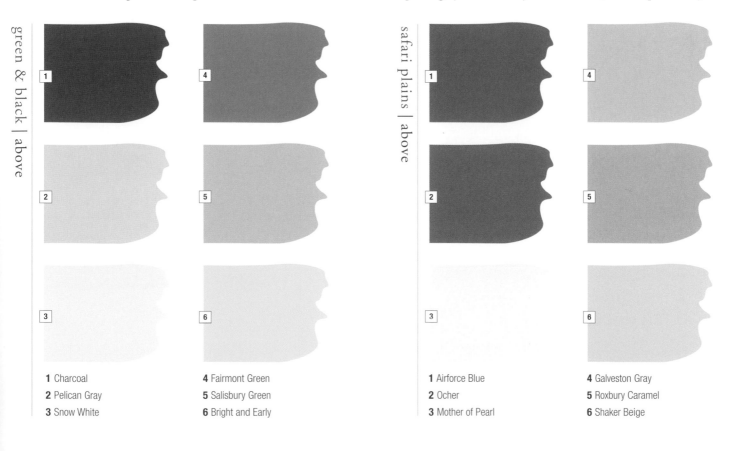

green & black | above

1 Charcoal

2 Pelican Gray

3 Snow White

4 Fairmont Green

5 Salisbury Green

6 Bright and Early

safari plains | above

1 Airforce Blue

2 Ocher

3 Mother of Pearl

4 Galveston Gray

5 Roxbury Caramel

6 Shaker Beige

panna cotta
& cappuccino

crème brûlée
cotton ball
string
jute
oatmeal
mascarpone
ivory
porcelain
café latte
vanilla
clotted cream
sesame seed
dairy milk
cornish cream
popcorn
cashmere
bleached beech
caramel
barley
mimosa
butterscotch
natural canvas
bone
papyrus
orchid
raw silk
limewash
calla lily
white hyacinth
alabaster
white truffle
madeira cake
wheatgrass
lily of the valley

ALL ABOUT OFF-WHITES

From barely-there off-whites to buttermilk, butterscotch, and biscotti, the off-white neutral tones are the holy grail of color palettes for me; they are soothing tones that are never out of date. Combine them with any number of similar and harmonious tones and you will never be disappointed, as they look beautiful under most lights and create palettes that are wonderfully warming and comfortable. They have the ability to work particularly well in contemporary spaces, yet never look out of place in pared-down country homes.

Nearly all decorators cite a particular off-white among their personal favorites in any little black book of decorating secrets. When it comes to creating cool but calm interiors, these are undemanding yet stunning colors. Relatively easy to choose and widely available, they are popular to work with. They are among the colors I truly love to live and decorate with, and I simply revel in their understated elegance.

Off-white, like black, performs differently than other colors in the way that it reflects and absorbs light. White will reflect almost all other colors, so be aware of this when choosing colors to go with it. You may not want a pale yellow, for instance, to be projected across a room and cast unflattering light. If you are in a cold northern light, it is best to choose an off-white that contains a higher proportion of raw umber for a subtle fawn or taupe color slant.

Creating a palette with such divine, elusive shades is both a pleasure and a challenge. The uninitiated may think, "Surely off-white is just dirty white?" Wrong. There are at least as many shades of white and off-white as there are days in a year, and some innovative paint companies, including Fine Paints of Europe and Farrow & Ball, have created their own palettes consisting solely of off-whites. They have sourced and refined a useful collection of subtle shades that are suitable for many different color-tinged neutral stories from shades that mix white with tinges of gray, brown, red, green and blue. These are the shades that are more readily mixed into white to provide the richer, warmer off-whites.

Getting the white right is important if you want a room to be warm and welcoming rather than drab with a gray cast. When you look around any paint shop you will realize just how many shades of off-white there are and how each one has its own subtle color balance within it. Gather together a collection of different off-white palettes and get used to looking at off-whites as colors within colors. This way you can quickly identify which palette they have a natural affinity with.

The most useful "dirty whites" often have a tiny element of raw umber in their base. This is a natural, brown clay pigment that provides a beige cast to pure white paint. Gray-whites are achieved by combining white with a stronger element of deeper umber, while an increase of both elements will result in a mole color.

There is a reason why the once dreadfully ubiquitous magnolia was as popular as it was. It was tinged with a particularly warm yellow ocher that made a room welcoming but inoffensive, neutral but bland. Warmer neutrals are the biscotti and buttermilk shades that include hints of yellow and brown, while cool neutrals include the pure whites of ricotta verging on the gray-green. These welcoming shades, combined with black and white and textured tones of toffee and gilt, have a still serenity to them, in a carefully chosen tableau of colors that create delicious harmony and an easy smartness.

The perfect off-whites step on the toes of true colors, but don't intrude into definite color statements. From cow's milk to cappuccino, they provide nuance rather than drama, notes rather than a full symphony.

ALABASTER

BUTTER CHURN

"Used singularly with unyielding textures and hidden patterns, these breezy, soft, and creamy whites entice you to explore beyond your first glance. These are unspoken and sometimes misinterpreted backdrops, but without them our favorite hues may otherwise go unnoticed." JACKIE JORDAN, DIRECTOR OF COLOR MARKETING, SHERWIN-WILLIAMS

NATURAL CANVAS

CAFÉ LATTE

LILY OF THE VALLEY

BLEACHED BEECH

USING OFF-WHITES Off-whites are everywhere, sometimes noticeable, sometimes blending into the background of a space where stronger colors take center stage. It's hard to go wrong when experimenting with and combining these gentle shades of linen, string, and latte, but layering them tone on tone, from the palest to the darkest, will add visual interest. Effortlessly elegant, they are versatile shades that can be kept subtle or enlivened with striking accent colors.

Natural surfaces are the perfect companions to these shades. Wood, stone, glass, and granite are all materials that provide texture, pattern, and deeper neutral shades in an off-white scheme. But beware, because sometimes so many natural tones in one space can look a bit bland if they are piled on top of one another in haphazard fashion. Make sure to choose about three or four base colors and use them on a variety of surfaces for the best effect. Use fabrics that echo an architectural feature, or match the wall color with accessories such as rugs and throws.

Rich but subtle accent earth colors such as Pompeii red, terra-cotta, and cocoa are the sensible deeper-toned companions for the base palette. To add some vigor to the palette, throw in some turquoise or shots of lime. Floors are important in an all-white scheme. Wooden floors—whether natural oak boards, a deep nut-brown painted floor, or boards painted in a white colorwash or limed—are the perfect anchor for white spaces. Experiment with gloss surfaces or deep, light-absorbing paint colors to provide additional texture and sheen.

Off-whites work in almost every room of the house, but are particularly smart in living rooms, bedrooms, and bathrooms, where their neutral elegance allows furniture, bedlinen, or chrome detailing to add extra layers of texture and

From the barely there tones of ricotta and mascarpone to the richer dairy shades of buttermilk and cappuccino, off-whites are the warm neutrals that never fail to create a welcome.

color to a scheme. Use them in gloss form on woodwork and floors for a crisp sheen in a totally white space or to provide glamorous definition where walls are in quite strong colors.

Off-whites are as perfectly at home in small spaces, where they blur the boundaries of confining walls, as they are in generous, light-filled rooms, where they infuse the space with an ethereal quality. In small spaces keep to one white or off-white. In larger spaces you can use a variety of whites and introduce a number of natural textures, too, for a layered approach. Use a number of different off-white shades on doors, windows and architectural detailing, then introduce shades of, say, linen, jute, and string across a number of surfaces such as rugs, upholstery, pillows, and throws.

When choosing colors to accompany off-whites, remember that adding white to a pure shade will produce a tint that lightens the overall color, so this is a good way to create a color you know will be sympathetic to the off-white. Adding gray to a pure hue changes the base color to a gray-toned version of it, for instance a pale gray mole rather than chocolate brown or pale pinky beige. In this way you can manipulate the stronger colors in a room so that they complement the off-whites.

Whichever neutral direction you choose to go in, keep the base colors mixed with an essentially warm shade and you can't go wrong.

OPPOSITE TOP LEFT In an Helsinki apartment full of cold northern light, a careful choice of rose-tinged whites and a sleek glossy floor make this white space warm despite its location.

OPPOSITE TOP RIGHT Cool alabaster white walls are framed with an intricate stonework mantle and hearth. Animal prints in black and white and a nubbly rug soften the room but continue the palette.

OPPOSITE BOTTOM LEFT In Connecticut, designer Jeffrey Bilhuber lets the natural light become part of a breezy bleached white story. There is nothing so inspiring as the perfect off-white.

OPPOSITE BOTTOM RIGHT In this Atlanta living room, designed by Tim Hobby of Space, Tim has made delicate use of ivory, vanilla ice, and cookie shades to create an enchanting, understated glamour.

panna cotta & cappuccino | ricotta

panna cotta & cappuccino | ricotta

panna cotta & cappuccino | buttermilk

panna cotta & cappuccino | buttermilk

1	Cotton Ball	7	Jute
2	Orchid	8	String
3	Clotted Cream	9	Oatmeal
4	Mother of Pearl	10	Natural Canvas
5	Alabaster	11	Bone
6	Calla Lily	12	Mimosa

1	Papyrus	7	Crème Brûlée
2	Curd	8	Sesame Seed
3	Cow's Milk	9	Salmon White
4	Popcorn	10	Ambrosia
5	Lily of the Valley	11	Warm Blush
6	Vanilla	12	Butter Churn

panna cotta & cappuccino | biscotti

panna cotta & cappuccino | biscotti

Neutrals are the perfect colors to decorate with. Calm, sophisticated, and always reassuring, they are capable of providing a subtle backdrop or of taking central casting by storm.

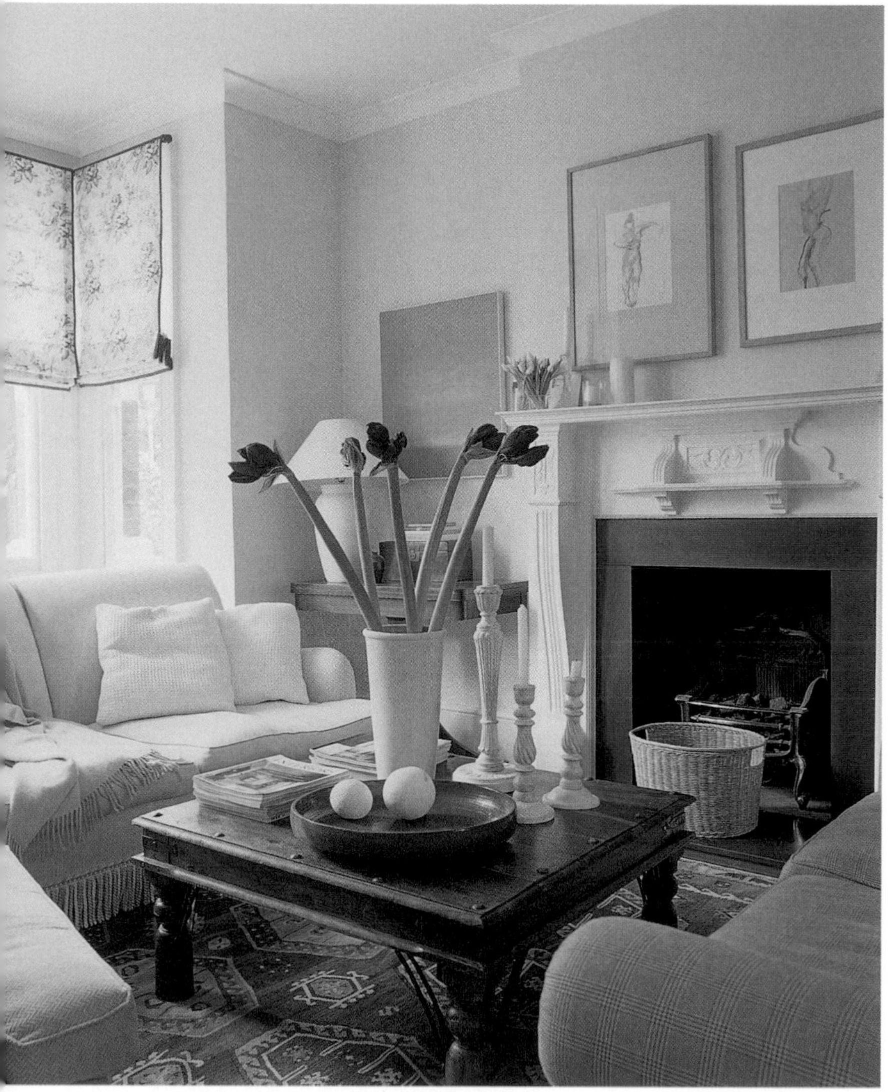

ABOVE Creamy wall tones of buttermilk provide a warming neutral backdrop for accent tones of faded coral and muted reds.

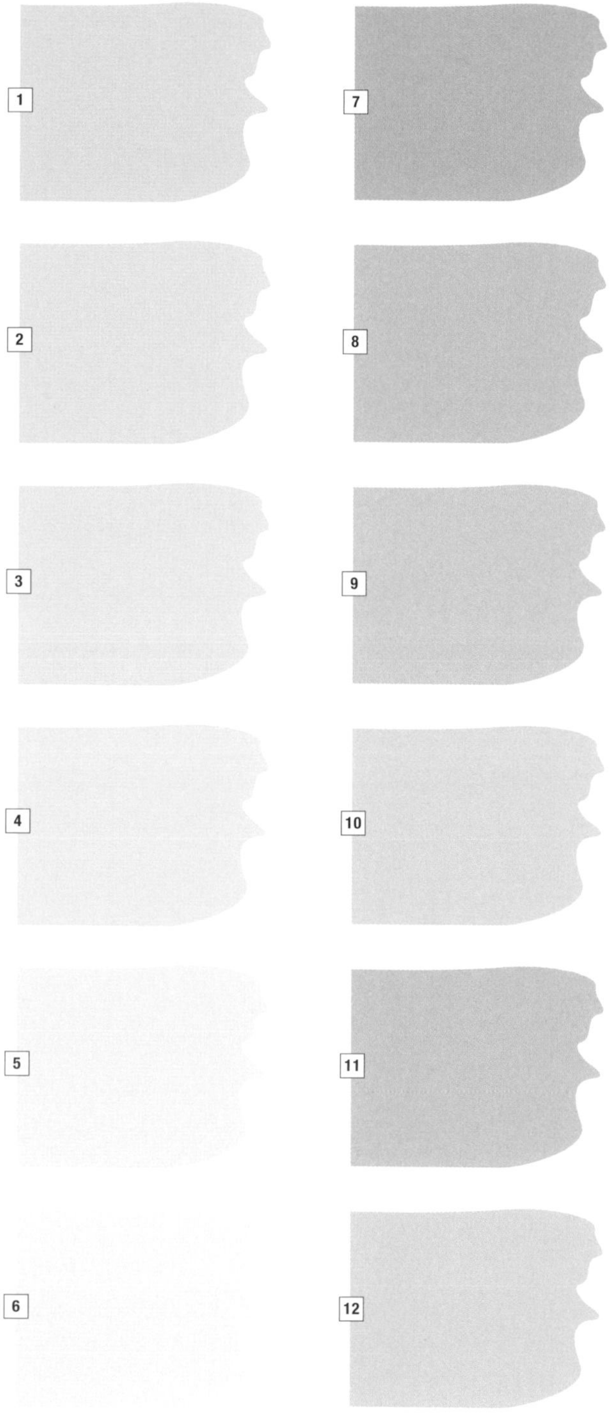

1 Barley
2 Natural Calico
3 Shortcake
4 Cornish Cream
5 White Truffle
6 Dairy Milk

7 Parchment
8 Café Latte
9 Cashmere
10 Bleached Beech
11 Oat Cake
12 Limewash

"To me the perfect white is very neutral, like my favorite, Benjamin Moore's Super White. I like whites that give space a sense of architecture without decorating it. A pure, untainted white creates the best plain canvas that I can create my rooms against."

VICENTE WOLF

THIS PAGE Creamy whites are always a wise choice for kitchen cupboards, bringing some dairy elegance to the space. On built-in wooden closets choose matte paint, but on cabinets it can be fun to experiment with gloss surfaces that shoot light back into the space.

OPPOSITE Successful off-whites are those that blend in thoroughly so that the space feels neither cold nor overly stark. Soften the atmosphere by introducing a variety of surfaces and finishes such as glass light fittings, or a glossy tabletop.

ricotta

Put a barely-there off-white next to a pure brilliant white, especially under a natural light source, and you will be amazed at the difference in tone. What can be described as white in a bright Caribbean light can look almost gray in cold northern light, so it is important to get the white right before you cover a room with it. The pale whites of ricotta and mascarpone, bone white and white truffle, are great "pale dairy" colors that are oh-so-subtle yet bathe a space in warm, natural light. Combine them in matte and gloss finishes for a perfect neutral marriage that allows surfaces to interact with one another and lets the light to dance around a room. These pale milky whites make good accent colors on woodwork and furniture for stronger shades in a room. Team bone whites with weathered grays, faded greens, rosy reds, pale lilacs or strong blues for the best effect. They will both highlight the colors and provide delicate definition. Introduce texture in the form of sisal matting, loose linen covers, and glossy woodwork, on walls or floors, to add further levels of visual interest.

Alternatively, you can bathe a whole room in porcelain tones for an all-white story that is surprisingly restful, particularly when accented with black detailing or touches of warm wood. Barely-there whites can be restful but smart, informal but elegant. Use them in kitchens for a clean, fresh look, or in living rooms where a level of understated elegance is required.

1 Clotted Cream

2 Chalk Pit

3 Pewter

4 Yellow Flower

5 Billowy Down

6 Cactus Flower

spring colors Rich

ricotta walls are simply stunning in company with palest celadon, sunflower and lemon yellow, and Swedish blue. A fresh, invigorating palette, this scheme is impossible to tire of, whatever the season.

lilac linen
An urban London home is bathed in light thanks to warm ricotta tones that are varied by one or two shades on walls, woodwork, and cornicing. Textured sisal flooring in natural colors and honey-colored incidental furniture mix well with lilac linen on the pillows and neutral furnishings.

1 Alabaster
2 Clotted Cream
3 Beige Sand
4 Lavender Blue
5 Wild Orchid
6 Exotic Red

"I like obsessive continuity in color. I paint walls, ceilings, and woodwork all the same in matte paint and high baseboards the same color in gloss. I prefer off-white colors" MIMMI O'CONNELL

THIS PAGE Soft buttery creams may look white but actually comprise a fair amount of red-tinged pigments to provide a subtle warm feel.

OPPOSITE Rich buttermilk cabinets are perfect for simple country-style kitchens, where oak wood floors and countertops team beautifully with the natural shades and textures.

buttermilk

The creamy tones of buttermilk, from soft wheat to crème brûlée, have faint tinges of yellow. These are in fact brownish tones formed by varying the intensities of the natural yellow ocher pigment that lends the color value. The resulting color is a warm off-white that never looks stark, even in northern light. These warm dairy shades of butter, ivory, and creamy milk work wonderfully well with rich oak tones, shades of royal blue, and ocher-sand tones. Schemes can be pushed towards a Provençal and Mediterranean feel, a muted take on a red and white theme, or else a traditional and enduring food-inspired chocolate and cream palette. Buttermilk and deep brown make up a pleasing and reassuring palette that is endlessly versatile for any room where natural materials and colors are present.

Deep corals and faded reds also look splendid with these tones—think peaches and cream. Navy blues conjure the nautical, while celery greens mixed with buttery tones create a sense of nature. Combine them with other neutrals such as earthy moles and taupes, wax-candle dairy shades, and spicy cinnamon or ginger tones. Buttermilk shades add depth, so use them in spaces where an enveloping feel is required, in kitchens and bedrooms, for instance. Particularly suited to the northern hemisphere, they perform the same function there as pure white in sunnier places, providing a perfect backdrop against which stronger colors can perform.

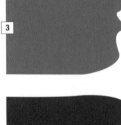

1 Curd
2 Winter Snow
3 Dark Oak
4 Deep Rose
5 Mauve Mist
6 Mauve Sable

strawberries & cream

A palette comprised of a wall color that could be magnolia by another name provides a calming backdrop for off-white three-quarter paneled walls and seating. Elements of strawberry crush on the rug, pillows, and curtain detailing lend interest and impact to the room.

buttercup & mole This neutral

story embraces the smudgy browns of fallen trees, stormy skies, and rich
buttermilk in the patterned curtains and picked up elsewhere in the room.
These balanced tones create a fresh and natural scheme that works
as well for the country as it would for the coast.

1 Lily of the Valley
2 Stoneground
3 Allspice
4 Blueberry
5 Paper White
6 French Horn

"No color works in isolation, and finding a new combination of colors that look wonderful together can be both rewarding and exciting. A subtle variation of color is an effective way to unite all the architectural elements of a room, which are frequently painted white through habit or un-adventure." DAVID OLIVER, THE PAINT LIBRARY

THIS PAGE Faded ice cream colors make perfect partners for oaten walls. These soft neutrals are both fresh and fetching in a quaint, period kitchen decorated with creamware serving plates.

OPPOSITE A marvelous array of wheat, biscuit, and beige gives this bedroom a smart, airy feel. Distressed paintwork on the wardrobe and a pleasing textured window shade add layers of interest to the palette.

biscotti

These caramel-toned neutrals are like the little black dress of the panna cotta palette, capable of being accessorized to make a grand statement, or of acting alone in an elegant class of their own. Versatile but never boring, they are a clear asset in rooms where natural light is limited, providing a neutral but not dull palette. Embolden these wheaten shades with dashes of lacquer red or jungle green to bring attention to them, or use harmonious tones of taupe, butterscotch, camel, and cappuccino for a toffee-tinged space. These deeper neutral tones are often tinted with browns and pinks that give them their natural warmth and allow colors other than pure latte to emanate from their surfaces. Natural surfaces and

fabrics such as velvet, suede, leather, and animal prints are perfectly at home in this color range. For accents, introduce elements of honey tones in the shape of brass lampstands, gilt mirrors, or candlesticks, and caramel-tinged sheepskin for layers of texture and reflective surfaces. Delicate, pale china in creamy tones of palest primrose and faded rose have their colors accented and enhanced by biscotti shades, particularly when applied to walls as a colorwash.

Biscotti colors work well in any room, but always provide a crisp edge in bathrooms, living rooms, bedrooms, and hallways. Their raw-umber–edged tones work in any kind of light and in any style of interior, whether country or contemporary, in a limited or a generous space.

1 Parchment
2 Golden Wheat
3 Green Pearl
4 Field Green
5 Mocha Express
6 Pale Primrose

cappuccino screen A single

feature wall in cappuccino tones breaks up a multi-purpose space of cool
linen colors, screening the staircase while also becoming a focal point in
the color scheme. A floor-to-ceiling statement picked out in this way
also provides the illusion of additional height.

fade to gray
This bedroom designed by Luigi Esposito combines a simple black and white palette for the furniture and bed linen with a delightful faux-suede wall in toasty jute tones. Its broken texture softens the darker black plains in the room.

fields of barley
A combination of delicate stripes, checks, and florals, clotted cream woodwork, and toffee notes is easy on the eye, creating a soft and welcoming atmosphere. These glorious tones succeed in being luxurious but still informal.

fade to gray | above

fields of barley | above

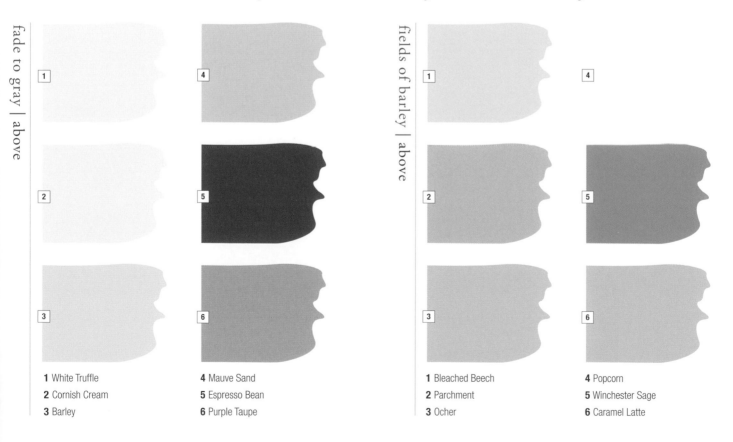

1 White Truffle   **4** Mauve Sand
2 Cornish Cream   **5** Espresso Bean
3 Barley   **6** Purple Taupe

1 Bleached Beech   **4** Popcorn
2 Parchment   **5** Winchester Sage
3 Ocher   **6** Caramel Latte

Sources for paint colors

SUNSHINE & CITRUS

PAGE 23
Provence Benjamin Moore Yellow Brick Road 349; Paint & Paper Library Chinese Emperor **Key Lime** Benjamin Moore Majestic Yellow 355; Sherwin-Williams 6691 Glitzy Gold **Stoneground** Benjamin Moore Traditional Yellow, Farrow & Ball Farrow's Cream 67 **Maize** Benjamin Moore Sunflower Fields 174; Sherwin-Williams 6678 Sunflower **Gold** Benjamin Moore Sunflower 2019-30; Sherwin-Williams 6889 Stirring Orange **Saffron** Benjamin Moore Citrus Blast 2018-30; Sherwin-Williams 6894 Forceful Orange

PAGE 26 LEMON
1 Cadmium Yellow Benjamin Moore Sun Kissed Yellow 2022-20; Sherwin-Williams 6903 Cheerful **2 Provence** Benjamin Moore Yellow Brick Road 349; Paint & Paper Library Chinese Emperor **3 Citrus Zest** Benjamin Moore Golden Orchards 329; Sherwin-Williams 6906 Citrus **4 Sundance** Benjamin Moore Bold Yellow 336; Sherwin-Williams 6907 Forsythia **5 Gilt Edge** Benjamin Moore Pure Joy 327; Sherwin-Williams 6910 Daisy **6 Pale Primrose** Benjamin Moore Lemon Grass 339; Sherwin-Williams 6909 Lemon Twist **7 Canary Yellow** Benjamin Moore Bright Gold 371; Sherwin-Williams 6699 Crispy Gold **8 Lemon Drop** Benjamin Moore Yellow Hibiscus 357; Sherwin-Williams 6698 Kingdom Gold **9 Key Lime** Benjamin Moore Majestic Yellow 355; Sherwin-Williams 6691 Glitzy Gold **10 Yellow Roses** Benjamin Moore Yellow Roses 353; Sherwin-Williams 6697 Nugget **11 Sunkissed** Benjamin Moore Fun in the Sun 358; Fine Paints of Europe SK23 **12 Butter Yellow** Benjamin Moore Falling Star 351; Farrow & Ball Lancaster Yellow 249

PAGE 27 SAND
1 Pampas Benjamin Moore Lion Heart 306; Paint & Paper Library Loyal Wheat **2 Cornfield** Benjamin Moore Country Comfort 305; Paint & Paper Library Clotted Cream **3 Barleytwist** Benjamin Moore Crowne Hill Yellow 312; Paint & Paper Library Hathaway **4 Soft Clay** Benjamin Moore Squish-Squash 311; Farrow & Ball Dayroom Yellow 233 **5 Wheaten** Benjamin Moore Popcorn Kernel 310; Paint & Paper Library Ivory III **6 Creamery** Benjamin Moore Halifax Cream 344; Paint & Paper Library Chalk I **7 Tangiers** Benjamin Moore Myan Gold 175; Sherwin-Williams 6370 Saucy Gold **8 Maize** Benjamin Moore Sunflower Fields 174; Sherwin-Williams 6678 Sunflower **9 Mango** Benjamin Moore Happily ever After 173 ; Sherwin-Williams 6899 Nasturtium **10 Cheetah** Benjamin Moore Sunny Days 172, Farrow & Ball Babouche 223 **11 Desert Sand** Benjamin Moore Sweet Butter 171, Farrow & Ball Sudbury Yellow 51 **12 Stoneground** Benjamin Moore Traditional Yellow, Farrow & Ball Farrow's Cream 67

PAGE 27 SUNFLOWER
1 Marigold Benjamin Moore Mandarin Orange 2018-20; Sherwin-Williams 6895 Laughing Orange **2 Saffron** Benjamin Moore Citrus Blast 2018-30; Sherwin-Williams 6894 Foreceful Orange **3 Gold** Benjamin Moore Sunflower 2019-30; Sherwin-Williams 6889 Stirring Orange **4 Maple Syrup** Benjamin Moore Nacho Cheese 2018-40; Sherwin-Williams 6675 Afternoon **5 Summer Sunshine** Benjamin Moore American Cheese 2019-40; Farrow & Ball Print Room Yellow 69 **6 Parmigiana** Benjamin Moore Lemon Drop 2019-50; Sherwin-Williams 6897 Sundance **7 Pumpkin** Benjamin Moore Desert Sunset 2155-10; Sherwin-Williams 6657 Amber Wave **8 Toscana** Benjamin Moore Gold Mine 2155-20; Sherwin-Williams 6887 Navel **9 Butternut Squash** Benjamin Moore Yellow Marigold 2155-30; Sherwin-Williams 6671 Curry **10 Honey** Benjamin Moore Semolina 2155-40; Paint & Paper Library Loyal Wheat; Sherwin-Williams 6663 Saffron Thread **11 Corn** Benjamin Moore Suntan Yellow 2155-50; Paint & Paper Library Pale Orlando **12 Buckwheat** Benjamin Moore Cream Yellow 2155-60; Paint & Paper Library Straw 1

PAGE 30 COUNTRY RETREAT
1 Sunkissed Benjamin Moore Fun in the Sun 358; Fine Paints of Europe SK23 **2 White Truffle** Benjamin Moore Powder Sand OC-113; Sherwin-Williams 0051 Classic Ivory **3 Cornflower Blue** Benjamin Moore Watertown 818; Farrow & Ball Pitch Blue 220 **4 Wedgwood Blue** Benjamin Moore Windmill Wings 2067-60; Farrow & Ball Lulworth Blue 89 **5 Leather Chair** Benjamin Moore Old Canal 1132; Sherwin-Williams 7725 Yearling **6 Swedish Gray** Benjamin Moore Shale 861; Paint & Paper Library Boudoir

PAGE 30 GREEN ACCENT
1 Citrus Zest Benjamin Moore Golden Orchards 329; Sherwin-Williams 6906 Citrus **2 Limewash** Benjamin Moore Spring in Aspen 954; Paint & Paper Library Suede 1 **3 Historic Green** Farrow & Ball Lichen 19; Fine Paints of Europe SK18 **4 Chinese Teal** Fine Paints of Europe AR-17; Benjamin Moore Captivating Teal 649 **5 Light Latte** Benjamin Moore Clear Field 1159; Paint & Paper Library Coral IV **6 Deep Mahogany** Benjamin Moore North Creek Brown 1001; Fine Paints of Europe SK-35

PAGE 31 BREEZY LIVING
1 Sundance Benjamin Moore Bold Yellow 336; Sherwin-Williams 6907 Forsythia **2 White Truffle** Benjamin Moore Powder Sand OC-113; Sherwin-Williams 0051 Classic Ivory **3 Mystical Powers** Benjamin Moore Mystical Powers 901; Paint & Paper Library Oak I **4 Faded Grass** Benjamin Moore Spring Dust 2150-40; Fine Paints of Europe SK-16 **5 Mocha Magic** Benjamin Moore Mountain Retreat 1176; Fine Paints of Europe LP-9 **6 Red Brick Wall** Benjamin Moore Fire Dance 2171-20: Paint & Paper Library Bettlenut

PAGE 35 COOL PROVENCE
1 Wheaten Benjamin Moore Popcorn Kernel 310; Paint & Paper Library Ivory III **2 Salmon White** Benjamin Moore Sheer Pink 894; Paint & Paper Library Coral I **3 Historic Provence** Benjamin Moore Yin Yang 824; Farrow & Ball Pitch Blue 220 **4 Steel Gray** Benjamin Moore Whispering Wind 1416; Fine Paints of Europe SK-27 **5 Antique Rose** Benjamin Moore Antique Rose 2173-40; Paint & Paper Library Roben's Honour **6 Pale Petal** Benjamin Moore Pale Petal 1178; Paint & Paper Library Foundation

PAGE 35 FIELD OF SAND
1 Cheetah Benjamin Moore Sunny Days 172; Farrow & Ball Babouche 223 **2 Parchment** Benjamin Moore Antique Parchment 959; Paint & Paper Library Paper IV **3 Tomato** Benjamin Moore Habanero Pepper 1306; Farrow & Ball Blazer 212 **4 Berry Red** Benjamin Moore My Valentine 1330; Farrow & Ball Rectory Red 217 **5 Naranja** Benjamin Moore Sharp Cheddar 2017-20; Francesca's Paints Louise's Orange **6 Bowling Green** Benjamin Moore Richmond Green 553; Francesca's Paints Classic Pesto

PAGE 38 SUNSHINE SPECTRUM
1 Summer Sunshine Benjamin Moore American Cheese 2019-40; Farrow & Ball Print Room Yellow 69 **2 Butternut Squash** Benjamin Moore Yellow Marigold 2155-30; Sherwin-Williams 6671 Curry **3 Beige Sand** Benjamin Moore Shabby Chic 1018; Sherwin-Williams 7712 Townhouse Tan **4 Venetian Sunset** Benjamin Moore Adobe Orange 2171-30; Francesca's Paints Rebecca Red **5 Bright Fuchsia** Benjamin Moore Pink Corsage 1349; Paint & Paper Library Elizabethan Red **6 Earthworks** Benjamin Moore Georgian Brick HC-50; Farrow & Ball Picture Gallery Red 42

PAGE 39 CHIC ADOBE
1 Marigold Benjamin Moore Mandarin Orange 2018-20; Sherwin-Williams 6895 Laughing Orange **2 Brown Sugar** Benjamin Moore Maple Sugar; Farrow & Ball Sand 45 **3 Pumice** Benjamin Moore Pink Coastal Cottage 1164; Paint & Paper Library Coral II **4 New White** Farrow & Ball New White 59; Paint & Paper Library Ivory 1 **5 Texas Rose** Benjamin Moore Texas Rose 2092-40; Farrow & Ball Porphry Pink 49 **6 Mississippi Mud** Benjamin Moore Mississippi Mud 2114-20; Farrow & Ball Mahogany 36

CRANBERRY & ORANGE

PAGE 43
Rose Garden Benjamin Moore Glamour Pink 2006-40; Martha Stewart Colors Jelly Bean MS006 **Cotton Candy** Benjamin Moore Bermuda Breeze 1345; Ralph Lauren French Pink IB49 **Tuscan Pink** Benjamin Moore Blush Tone 2000-50; Sherwin-Williams 6312 Redbud **Nectarine** Benjamin Moore Carrot Stick 2016-30; Sherwin-Williams 6886 Invigorate **Mulberry** Benjamin Moore Cherry Wine 2080-30; Paint & Paper Library Elizabethan Red **Moroccan Red** Benjamin Moore Tangerine Dream 2012-30; Sherwin-Williams 6875 Gladiolar

PAGE 46 ROSE
1 Jaipur Benjamin Moore Razzle Dazzle 1348; Sherwin-Williams 6840 Exuberant Pink **2 Venetian Rose** Benjamin Moore Pink Ladies 1347; Francesca's Paints Rose Bank **3 Pink Lipstick** Benjamin Moore Island Sunset 1346; Sherwin-Williams 6579 Gala Pink **4 Pink Dream** Benjamin Moore Misted Rose 1339; Ralph Lauren Key Largo IB54 **5 Cotton Candy** Benjamin Moore Bermuda Breeze 1345; Ralph Lauren French Pink IB49 **6 Sugar Almond** Benjamin Moore Rose Garden 1353; Martha Stewart Colors Party Streamer MS010 **7 Tuscan Red** Benjamin Moore Coral Bronze 1298: Martha Stewart Colors Chinese Lacquer Red MS027 **8 Rose Garden** Benjamin Moore Glamour Pink 2006-40 Martha Stewart Colors Jelly Bean MS006 **9 Plaster Pink** Benjamin Moore Venetian Rose 1292; Martha Stewart Colors Gerbera Daisy MS007 **10 Brick Pink** Benjamin Moore Pink Punch 2006-50; Martha Stewart Colors Grosgrain MS008 **11 Strawberry Milkshake** Benjamin Moore Authentic Pink 2006-60; Martha Stewart Colors Flower Petal Pink MS035 **12 Baby Pink** Benjamin Moore Pink Fairy 2006-70; Martha Stewart Colors Tutu MS012

PAGE 47 FLAME
1 Tangerine Dream Benjamin Moore Electric Orange 2015-10; Sherwin-Williams 6884 Orange **2 Paprika** Benjamin Moore Startling Orange 2016-10; Sherwin-Williams 6882 Daredevil **3 Carrot Stick** Benjamin Moore Orange Juice 2017-10; Sherwin-Williams 6884 Obstinate Or-ange **4 Nectarine** Benjamin Moore Carrot Stick 2016-30; Sherwin-Williams 6886 Invigorate **5 Ocher Sand** Benjamin Moore Marmalade 2016-40; Sherwin-Williams 6644 Marigold **6 Peach** Benjamin Moore Melon Popsicle 2016-50; Sherwin-Williams 6654 Surprise Amber **7 Cadmium** Benjamin Moore Tawny Day Lily 2012-10; Sherwin-Williams 6867 Fireworks **8 Crimson** Benjamin Moore Flame 2012-20; Sherwin-Williams 6870 Ablaze **9 Moroccan Red** Benjamin Moore Tangerine Dream 2012-30; Sherwin-Williams 6875 Gladiola **10 Coral** Benjamin Moore Summer Sun Pink 2012-40; Marta Stewart Colors Peony Orange MS032 **11 Freckle Flesh** Benjamin Moore Perky Peach 2012-50; Sherwin-Williams 6878 Animated Coral **12 Faded Rose** Benjamin Moore Creamy Peach 2012-60; Sherwin-Williams 6877 Inner Child

PAGE 47 REDCURRANT
1 Racing Red Benjamin Moore Red 2000-10; Sherwin-Williams 6868 Real Red **2 Chili Pepper** Benjamin Moore Tricycle Red 2000-20; Sherwin-Williams 6866 Hearttthrob **3 Poppy** Benjamin Moore Red Tulip 2000-30; Ralph Lauren Aruba Pink IB52 **4 Raspberry Mousse** Benjamin Moore Strawberry Shortcake 2000-40: Sherwin-Williams 6313 Kirsch Red **5 Tuscan Pink** Benjamin Moore Blush Tone 2000-50; Sherwin-Williams 6312 Redbud **6 Silky Pink** Benjamin Moore Light Chiffon Pink 2000-60; Sherwin-Williams 6583 In The Pink **7 French Claret** Benjamin Moore Raspberry Truffle 2080-10: Ralph Lauren Amalfi Red IB60 **8 Rich Burgundy** Benjamin Moore Confederate 2080-20; Farrow & Ball Rectory Red 217 **9 Mulberry** Benjamin Moore Cherry Wine 2080-30; Paint & Paper Library Elizabethan Red **10 Pomegranate** Benjamin Moore Wild Pink 2080-40; Ralph Lauren Paint Belmont Pink IB50 **11 Sherbet Pink** Benjamin Moore Posy Pink 2080-6012; Ralph Lauren Mission Wildflower IB53 **12 Antique Rose** Benjamin Moore Aztec Lily 2080-70; Paint & Paper Library Oyster Lily

PAGE 50 TWO-TONE ROSE
1 Strawberry Milkshake Benjamin Moore Authentic Pink 2006-60; Martha Stewart Colors Flower Petal Pink MS035 **2 Antique Rose** Benjamin Moore Aztec Lily 2080 70; Paint & Paper Library Oyster Lily **3 Military Uniform** Benjamin Moore Stratford Blue 831; Sherwin-Williams 6251 Outerspace **4 Purple Heart** Benjamin Moore Purple Heart 1406; Sherwin-Williams 6818 Valiant Violet **5 Lilac Gray** Benjamin Moore French Lilac 1403; Sherwin-Williams 6822 Wisteria **6 Gustavian** Benjamin Moore Sunrise 829; Sherwin-Williams 6522 Sporty Blue

PAGE 51 LA VIE EN ROSE
1 Venetian Rose Benjamin Moore Pink Ladies 1347; Sherwin-Williams 6579 Gala Pink **2 Mimosa** Benjamin Moore Cloud Cover OC-25; Farrow & Ball Strong White 2001 **3 Gustavian Gray** Benjamin Moore Manor Blue 1627; Sherwin-Williams 6256 Serious Gray **4 Evening Dove** Benjamin Moore Evening Dove 2128-30; Sherwin-Williams 6989 Domino **5 Kiwi** Benjamin Moore Kiwi 544;Sherwin-Williams 6718 Overt Green **6 Lavender Blue** Benjamin Moore Snugglepuss 1405; Sherwin-Williams 6551 Purple Passage

PAGE 55 FLAME HEAVEN
1 Cadmium Benjamin Moore Tawny Day Lily 2012-10; Sherwin-Williams 6867 Fireworks **2 Yellow Roses** Benjamin Moore Yellow Roses 353; Sherwin-Williams 6697 Nugget **3 Butter Yellow** Benjamin Moore Falling Star 351; Farrow & Ball Lancaster Yellow 249 **4 Apple Orchard** Benjamin Moore Malachy Green 419; Sherwin-Williams 6922 Outrageous Green **5 Softened Violet** Benjamin Moore Softened Violet 1420; Sherwin-Williams 6824 Forget-me-not **6 Tundra Ice** Benjamin Moore Baby's Breath OC-62; Sherwin-Williams 7551 Greek Villa

PAGE 55 TANGERINE DREAM
1 Tangerine Dream Benjamin Moore Electric Orange 2015 10; Sherwin-Williams 6884 Orange **2 Vanilla** Benjamin Moore White Blush 904; Farrow & Ball White Tie 2002 **3 Nautical White** Benjamin Moore Misty Air OC-44; Sherwin-Williams 6157 Favorite Tan **4 Cream** Farrow & Ball Cream 44; Francesca's Paints Sikhara Stone **5 Ryan Red** Benjamin Moore Ryan Red 1314; Sherwin-Williams 6601 Tanager **6 Copper Clay** Benjamin Moore Copper Clay 2172-10; Sherwin-Williams 6328 Fireweed

PAGE 58 FEEL THE HEAT
1 Racing Red Benjamin Moore Red 2000-10; Sherwin-Williams 6868 Real Red **2 Charcoal** Benjamin Moore Cheating Heart 1617; Sherwin-Williams 6258 Tricorn Black **3 Paprika** Benjamin Moore Startling Orange 2016-10; Sherwin-Williams 6882 Daredevil **4 Tuscan Pink** Benjamin Moore Blush Tone 2000-50; Sherwin-Williams 6312 Redbud **5 Salmon White** Benjamin Moore Sheer Pink 894; Sherwin-Williams 6323 Romance **6 Strawberry Milkshake** Benjamin Moore Authentic Pink 2006-60; Marta Stewart Colors Flower Petal Pink MS035

PAGE 59 MARRAKESH EXPRESS
1 Chili Pepper Benjamin Moore Tricycle Red 2000- 20; Sherwin-Williams 6866 Hearttthrob **2 Mother of Pearl** Benjamin Moore Swiss Coffee OC-45; Paint & Paper Library Sand I **3 Eggplant** Benjamin Moore Eggplant 1379; Sherwin-Williams 7577 Blackberry **4 Sloe Gin** Benjamin Moore Hot Lips 2077-30; Sherwin-Williams 6842 Forward Fuchsia **5 Imperial Yellow** Benjamin Moore Imperial Yellow 314; Sherwin-Williams 6899 Nasturtium **6 Pewter** Benjamin Moore Silent Night 1613; Sherwin-Williams 7655 Stamped Concrete

PAGE 59 HOT COALS
1 Rich Burgundy Benjamin Moore Confederate Red 2080-20; Farrow & Ball Rectory Red 217 **2 Chili Pepper** Benjamin Moore Tricycle Red 2000-20; Sherwin-Williams 6866 Hearttthrob **3 Parchment** Benjamin Moore Antique Parchment 959: Paint & Paper Library Paper IV **4 Silver Birch** Benjamin Moore Silver Bells 1458; Sherwin-Williams 2844 Roycroft Mist Gray **5 Wood Violet** Benjamin Moore Wood Violet 1428; Sherwin-Williams 6244 Naval **6 Oxford Gray** Benjamin Moore Oxford Gray 2128-40; Sherwin-Williams 7619 Labradorite

LILAC & PLUM

PAGE 63
Lilac Gray Benjamin Moore French Lilac 1403; Sherwin-Williams 6822 Wisteria **Iris** Benjamin Moore Charmed Violet 1398; Sherwin-Williams 6983 Fully Purple **Fig** Benjamin Moore Purple Rain 1386; Sherwin-Williams 6545 Majestic Purple **Sloe Gin** Benjamin Moore Hot Lips 2077-30; Sherwin-Williams 6842 Forward Fuchsia **Marshmallow** Benjamin Moore Bunny Nose 2074-60; Sherwin-Williams 6845 Child's Play **Boysenberry** Vintage Claret 1364; Sherwin-Williams 6300 Burgundy

PAGE 66 PARMA VIOLET
1 Deep Purple Benjamin Moore Fire and Ice 1392; Sherwin-Williams 6552 Dewberry **2 Iris** Benjamin Moore Charmed Violet 1398; Sherwin-Williams 6983 Fully Purple **3 Crème de Cassis** Benjamin Moore Naples Sunset 1391; Sherwin-Williams 6286 Mature Grape **4 Mauve Sunset** Benjamin Moore Hydrangea 1390; Sherwin-Williams 6285 Grape Harvest **5 French Hydrangea** Benjamin Moore Wishing Well 1389; Sherwin-Williams 0074 Radiant Lilac **6 Spring Lilac** Benjamin Moore Spring Lilac 1388; Paint & Paper Library Subtle Angel **7 Modern Mauve** Benjamin Moore Mauve Bauhaus 1407; Sherwin-Williams 6545 Majestic Purple **8 Purple Heart** Benjamin Moore Purple Heart 1406; Sherwin-Williams 6818 Valiant Violet **9 Lavender Blue** Benjamin Moore Snugglepuss 1405; Sherwin-Williams 6551 Purple Passage **10 Crocus** Benjamin Moore Crocus 1404; Sherwin-Williams 6557 Wood Violet **11 Lilac Gray** Benjamin Moore French Lilac 1403; Sherwin-Williams 6822 Wisteria **12 Mauve Alabaster** Benjamin Moore Spring Iris 1402; Sherwin-Williams 6834 Spangle

PAGE 66 GERANIUM
1 Rich Ruby Benjamin Moore Magenta 2077-10; 6300 Sherwin-Williams 6300 Burgundy **2 Bougainvillea** Benjamin Moore Gypsy Pink 2077-20; Sherwin-Williams 6566 Framboise **3 Sloe Gin** Benjamin Moore Hot Lips 2077-30; Sherwin-Williams 6842 Forward Fuchsia **4 Electric Pink** Benjamin Moore Spring Azalea 2077-40; Sherwin-Williams Exuberant Pink **5 Umbrian Rose** Benjamin Moore Pretty Pink 2077-50; Sherwin-Williams 6847 Ice Plant **6 Tea Rose** Benjamin Moore Valentine's Day 2077-60; Sherwin-Williams 6569 Childlike **7 Summer Plum** Benjamin Moore Summer Plum 2074-20; Francesca's Paints Jacaranda **8 Passionflower** Benjamin Moore Twilight Magenta 2074-30; Sherwin-Williams 6293 Fabulous Grape **9 Bright Lilac** Benjamin Moore Lilac Pink 2074-40; Sherwin-Williams 6978 Drama Violet **10 Princess Pink** Benjamin Moore Exotic Fuchsia 2074-50; Sherwin-Williams 6846 Prominent Pink **11 Marshmallow** Benjamin Moore Bunny Nose 2074-60; Sherwin-Williams 6845 Child's Play **12 Pink Peppermint** Benjamin Moore Easter Bonnet 2074-70; Sherwin-Williams 6561 Teaberry

PAGE 67 EGGPLANT
1 Blueberry Benjamin Moore Grappa 1393; Farrow & Ball Pelt 254 **2 Fig** Benjamin Moore Purple Rain 1386; Sherwin-Williams 6545 Majestic Purple **3 Plum Pie** Benjamin Moore Cupid's Dart 1385; Sherwin-Williams 6552 Dewberry **4 Faded Grape** Benjamin Moore Carolina Plum 1384; Sherwin-Williams 6558 Plummy **5 French Gray** Benjamin Moore Iris Bliss 1383; Sherwin-Williams 6557 Wood Violet **6 Violet Petal** Benjamin Moore Violet Petal 1382; Sherwin-Williams 6017 Intuitive **7 Grape** Benjamin Moore Bordeaux Red 1365; Sherwin-Williams 6020 Marooned **8 Boysenberry** Vintage Claret 1364; Sherwin-Williams 6300 Burgundy **9 Melrose Pink** Benjamin Moore Melrose Pink 1363; 6293 Sherwin-Williams Fabulous Grape **10 Cranberry Ice** Benjamin Moore Cranberry Ice 1362; Sherwin-Williams 6292 Berry Bush **11 Countryside Pink** Benjamin Moore 1361; Sherwin-Williams 6570 Haute Pink **12 Misty Rose** Benjamin Moore Misty Rose 1360; Sherwin-Williams 6568 Lighthearted Pink

PAGE 70 MULTI-LAYERED
1 Lilac Gray Benjamin Moore French Lilac 1403; Sherwin-Williams 6822 Wisteria **2 Mauve Sunset** Benjamin Moore Hydrangea 1390; Sherwin-Williams 6285 Grape Harvest **3 Mauve Finesse** Sherwin-Williams 7108 Pink Vibernum; Paint & Paper Library Plaster IV **4 Lime Twist** Benjamin Moore Lime Twist 425; Sherwin-Williams 6930 Laudable Lime **5 Celadon** Benjamin Moore Mountain View 583; Sherwin-Williams 6929 Witty Green **6 Spring Lilac** Benjamin Moore Spring Lilac 1388; Paint & Paper Library Subtle Angel

PAGE 70 KITCHEN ZING
1 Crocus Benjamin Moore Crocus 1404; Sherwin-Williams 6557 Wood Violet **2 Purple Heart** Benjamin Moore Purple Heart 1406; Sherwin-Williams 6818 Valiant Violet **3 Stainless Steel** Benjamin Moore Blue Lace 1625; Sherwin-Williams 6204 Sea Salt **4 Pure Apple** Benjamin Moore Killala Green 558; Sherwin-Williams 6931 Jolly Green **5 Shamrock** Benjamin Moore Luck of the Irish 588; Sherwin-Williams 6750 Kilkenny **6 Vanilla** Benjamin Moore White Blush 904; Farrow & Ball White Tie 2002

PAGE 71 COOL DINING
1 Lavender Blue Benjamin Moore Snugglepuss 1409; Sherwin-Williams 6551 Purple Passage **2 Cornflower Blue** Benjamin Moore Watertown 818; Sherwin-Williams 6803 Danube **3 Mint Tea** Benjamin Moore Scenic View 424; Sherwin-Williams 6717 Lime Rickey **4 Barley** Benjamin Moore Pale Moon OC-108; Farrow & Ball Hound Lemon 2 **5 Fig** Benjamin Moore Purple Rain 1386; Sherwin-Williams 6545 Majestic Purple **6 Sunset** Farrow & Ball Orangery 70; Sherwin-Williams 6677 Goldenrod

PAGE 74 CASA VIVA
1 Rich Ruby Benjamin Moore Magenta 2077-10; 6300 Sherwin-Williams 6300 Burgundy **2 Electric Pink** Benjamin Moore Spring Azalea 2077-40; Sherwin-Williams Exuberant Pink **3 Pine Sprigs** Benjamin Moore Pine Sprigs 423; Sherwin-Williams 6709 Gleeful **4 Pink Peppermint** Benjamin Moore Easter Bonnet 2074-70; Sherwin-Williams 6561 Teaberry **5 Blue Orchid** Benjamin Moore Blue Orchid 2069-50; Sherwin-Williams 6543 Soulful Blue **6 Mighty Aphrodite** Benjamin Moore Mighty Aphrodite 1397; Sherwin-Williams 6558 Plummy

PAGE 75 RICH IN PINK
1 Electric Pink Benjamin Moore Spring Azalea 2077-40; Sherwin-Williams Exuberant Pink **2 Rich Ruby** Benjamin Moore Magenta 2077-10; 6300 Sherwin-Williams 6300 Burgundy **3 Bright Lilac** Benjamin Moore Lilac Pink 2074-40; Sherwin-Williams 6978 Drama Violet **4 Cheetah** Benjamin Moore Sunny Days 172; Farrow & Ball Babouche 223 **5 Blueberry** Benjamin Moore Grappa 1393; Farrow & Ball Pelt 254 **6 Silver Mink** Benjamin Moore Silver Mink 1587; Sherwin-Williams 6249 Storm Cloud

PAGE 79 REGAL ELEGANCE
1 Plum Pie Benjamin Moore Cupid's Dart 1385; Sherwin-Williams 6552 Dewberry **2 Fig** Benjamin Moore Purple Rain 1386; Sherwin-Williams 6545 Majestic Purple **3 Chalk** Benjamin Moore Halo OC-46; Sherwin-Williams 0011 Crewel Tan **4 Currant Red** Benjamin Moore Currant Red 1323; Farrow & Ball Incarnadine 248 **5 Santa Clara** Benjamin Moore Santa Clara 753; Sherwin-Williams 6946 Surfer **6 Hummingbird Green** Benjamin Moore Hummingbird Green 2042-30; Sherwin-Williams 6987 Jitterbug Jade

PAGE 79 READING ROOM
1 Boysenberry Benjamin Moore Vintage Claret 1364; Sherwin-Williams 6300 Burgundy **2 Cranberry Ice** Benjamin Moore Cranberry Ice 1362; Sherwin-Williams 6292 Berry Bush **3 Papyrus** Benjamin Moore Antique White 909; Farrow & Ball Ringwold Ground 208 **4 Yellow Ground** Farrow & Ball Yellow Ground 218; Sherwin-Williams 6889 Stirring Orange **5 Deep Olive** Farrow & Ball Olive 13; Sherwin-Williams 6426 Basque Green **6 Blue Belle** Benjamin Moore Blue Belle 782; Sherwin-Williams 6955 Impromptu

SEA & SKY

PAGE 83
Mexico Benjamin Moore Bayberry Blue 790; Sherwin-Williams 6959

Blue Chip **Aquamarine** Benjamin Moore Dream I Can Fly 769; Sherwin-Williams 6951 Cote D'Azu **Poolside** Benjamin Moore Poolside 775; Sherwin-Williams 6509 Georgian Bay **Cobalt** Benjamin Moore Athens Blue 797; Sherwin-Williams 6804 Dignity Blue **Gunmetal Blue** Benjamin Moore Blue Heron 832; Sherwin-Williams 6517 Regatta **Military Uniform** Benjamin Moore Stratford Blue 831; Sherwin-Williams 6251 Outerspace

PAGE 86 SUMMER SKIES
1 Mexico Benjamin Moore Bayberry Blue 790; Sherwin-Williams 6959 Blue Chip **2 Kingfisher** Benjamin Moore Sea to Shining Sea 789; Sherwin-Williams 6795 Major Blue **3 Forget-me-Not** Benjamin Moore Aquarius 788; Sherwin-Williams 6802 Jacaranda **4 Rockpool** Benjamin Moore Grandma's Sweater 787; Sherwin-Williams 6953 Candid Blue **5 Wedgwood** Benjamin Moore Highland Breeze 786; Sherwin-Williams 6793 Bluebell **6 Delft** Benjamin Moore Morning Glory 785; Sherwin-Williams 6786 Cloudless **7 Aquamarine** Benjamin Moore Dream I Can Fly 769; Sherwin-Williams 6951 Cote D'Azur **8 Beach Shack** Benjamin Moore Atlantis Blue 798; Sherwin-Williams 6775 Briny **9 Turquoise** Benjamin Moore Graceful Sea 767; Sherwin-Williams 6787 Fountain **10 Shoreline** Benjamin Moore Delano Waters 766; Sherwin Williams 6949 Sllick Blue **11 Gray Day** Benjamin Moore Skyscraper 765; Sherwin-Williams 6944 Pool Blue **12 Duck Egg** Benjamin Moore Crystal Springs 764; Sherwin-Williams 6765 Spa

PAGE 87 OCEAN
1 Prussian Blue Benjamin Moore Blue Suede Shoes 798; Sherwin-Williams 6524 Commodore **2 Cobalt** Benjamin Moore Athens Blue 797; Sherwin-Williams 6804 Dignity Blue **3 Periwinkle** Nova Scotia Blue 796; Sherwin-Williams 6966 Blueblood **4 Faded Denim** Benjamin Moore Faded Denim 795; Sherwin-Williams 6801 Regale Blue **5 Cool Blue** Benjamin Moore Paradise View 794; Sherwin-Williams 68577 Undercool **6 Ice Blue** Benjamin Moore Mystical Blue 792; Sherwin-Williams 6792 Minor Blue **7 Midnight Sky** Benjamin Moore Summer Nights 777; Sherwin-Williams 6230 Rainstorm **8 Shaker Blue** Benjamin Moore Santa Monica Blue 776; Sherwin-Williams 6517 Regatta **9 Poolside** Benjamin Moore Poolside 775; Sherwin-Williams 6509 Georgian Bay **10 Cabina** Benjamin Moore I've Got the Blues 774; Sherwin-Williams 6782 Cruising **11 Athenian Blue** Benjamin Moore Athenian Blue 773; Sherwin-Williams 7606 Blue Cruise **12 Hawaiian Breeze** Benjamin Moore Hawaiian Breeze 772; Sherwin-Williams 6793 Bluebell

PAGE 87 STORMY
1 Midnight Blue Benjamin Moore Hale Navy HC-154; Farrow & Ball Railings 31 **2 Moonlight** Newburyport Blue Benjamin Moore HC-155; Sherwin-Williams 7076 Cyberspace **3 Deep Navy** Benjamin Moore Van Deusen Blue HC-156; Sherwin-Williams 6230 Rainstorm **4 Pebble Gray** Benjamin Moore Philipsburg Blue HC-159; Sherwin-Williams 7623 Cascades **5 Steely Sky** Van Courtland Blue HC-145; Sherwin-Williams 6223 Still Water **6 Wedgewood Gray** Benjamin Moore Wedgewood Gray HC-146; Sherwin-Williams 6214 Undersea **7 Evening Sky** Benjamin Moore Evening Sky 833; Sherwin-Williams 6992 Inkwell **8 Gunmetal Blue** Benjamin Moore Blue Heron 832; Sherwin-Williams 6517 Regatta **9 Military Uniform** Benjamin Moore Stratford Blue 831; Sherwin-Williams 6251 Outerspace **10 Harlequin Blue** Benjamin Moore Harlequin Blue 830; Sherwin-Williams 6235 Foggy Day **11 Gustavian** Benjamin Moore Sunrise 829; Sherwin-Williams 6522 Sporty Blue **12 Blue-Gray** Benjamin Moore Lake Placid 827; Sherwin-Williams 6225 Sleepy Blue

PAGE 90 RICH WOOD
1 Wedgwood Benjamin Moore Highland Breeze 786; Sherwin-Williams 6793 Bluebell **2 Plaster Pink** Benjamin Moore Venetian Rose 1292; Martha Stewart Colors Gerbera Daisy MS007 **3 Snow White** Benjamin Moore Snow White OC-66; Sherwin-Williams 6253 Olympus White **4 Walnut Tan** Benjamin Moore Vero Beach Tan 1085; Sherwin-Williams 6090 Java **5 Light Ocher** Benjamin Moore Concord Ivory HC-12; Sherwin-Williams 6655 Adventure Orange **6 Meadow Barley** Benjamin Moore French Manicure 1086; Sherwin-Williams 6646 Orange Blast

PAGE 90 MANHATTAN COOL
1 Shoreline Benjamin Moore Delano Waters 766; Sherwin Williams 6949 Sllick Blue **2 Cool Blue** Benjamin Moore Paradise View 794; Sherwin-Williams 68577 Undercool **3 Dirty White** Farrow & Ball Blackened 201; Sherwin-Williams 7006 Extra White **4 Florida Green** Benjamin Moore Floradale Isle 581; Sherwin-Williams 6741 Derbyshire **5 Springhill Green** Benjamin Moore Springhill Green 412; Sherwin-Williams 6922 Outrageous Green **6 Princess Pink** Benjamin Moore Exotic Fuchsia 2074-50; Sherwin-Williams 6846 Prominent Pink

PAGE 91 PROVENCAL DINING
1 Rockpool Benjamin Moore Grandma's Sweater 787; Sherwin-Williams 6953 Candid Blue **2 Kingfisher** Benjamin Moore Sea to Shining Sea 789; Sherwin-Williams 6795 Major Blue **3 Blue-Gray** Benjamin Moore Lake Placid 827; Sherwin-Williams 6225 Sleepy Blue **4 Ladybug Red** Benjamin Moore Ladybug Red 1322; Sherwin-Williams 6594 Poinsettia **5 Genuine Pink** Benjamin Moore Genuine Pink 2005-40; Sherwin-Williams 6312 Redbud **6 Moroccan Red** Benjamin Moore Tangerine Dream 2012 30; Sherwin-Williams 6875 Gladiola

PAGE 93 CHINA CORNER
1 Delft Benjamin Moore Morning Glory 785; Sherwin-Williams 6786 Cloudless **2 Gustavian** Benjamin Moore Sunrise 829; Sherwin-Williams 6522 Sporty Blue **3 Periwinkle** Nova Scotia Blue 796; Sherwin-Williams 6966 Blueblood **4 Cobalt** Benjamin Moore Athens Blue 797; Sherwin-Williams 6804 Dignity Blue **5 Butter Churn** Benjamin Moore Opal 891; Fine Paints of Europe SK-2 **6 Winchester Sage** Benjamin Moore Winchester Sage 628; Sherwin-Williams 6452 Inland

PAGE 93 COASTAL CALM
1 Wedgwood Benjamin Moore Highland Breeze 786; Sherwin-Williams 6793 Bluebell **2 Harlequin Blue** Benjamin Moore Harlequin Blue 830; Sherwin-Williams 6235 Foggy Day **3 Cashmere** Benjamin Moore Papaya 957; Sherwin-Williams 6667 Afterglow **4 Dove Wing** Benjamin Moore Dove Wing 960; Sherwin-Williams 6056 Polite White **5 Vermilion** Benjamin Moore Vermilion 2002-10; Sherwin-Williams 6601 Tanager **6 Marine Blue** Benjamin Moore Marine Blue 2059-10; Farrow & Ball Drawing Room Blue 253

PAGE 96 SPANISH MODERN
1 Prussian Blue Benjamin Moore Blue Suede Shoes 798; Sherwin-Williams 6524 Commodore **2 Winter Gates** Benjamin Moore Winter Gates AC-30; Fine Paints of Europe SK-32 **3 Silver Birch** Benjamin Moore Silver Bells 1458; Sherwin-Williams 2844 Roycroft Mist Gray **4 Secluded Beach** Benjamin Moore Secluded Beach 899; Shserwin-Williams 6674 Jonquil **5 Noisette** Benjamin Moore Wildnerness Cabin 1168; Sherwin-Williams 6656 Serape **6 Classic Brown** Benjamin Moore Classic Brown 2109-10; Sherwin-Williams 6006 Black Bean

PAGE 97 TURQUOISE TWIST
1 Athenian Blue Benjamin Moore Athenian Blue 773; Sherwin-Williams 7606 Blue Cruise **2 Delft** Benjamin Moore Morning Glory 785; Sherwin-Williams 6786 Cloudless **3 Ocher** Benjamin Moore Roasted Sesame Seed 2160-40; Sherwin-Williams 6360 Folksy Gold **4 Great White** Farrow & Ball Great White 2006; Sherwin-Williams 7539 Barcelona Beige **5 Greenfield Pumpkin** Benjamin Moore Greenfield Pumpkin HC-40; Sherwin-Williams 6097 Sturdy Brown **6 Roxbury Caramel** Benjamin Moore Roxbury Caramel HC-42; Sherwin-Williams 6117 Smokey Topaz

PAGE 100 WEDGWOOD BLUES
1 Gunmetal Blue Benjamin Moore Blue Heron 832; Sherwin-Williams 6517 Regatta **2 Gunmetal** Benjamin Moore Gentle Gray 1626; Sherwin-Williams 6476 Glimmer **3 Silver Birch** Benjamin Moore Silver Bells 1458; Sherwin-Williams 2844 Roycroft Mist Gray **4 Plum Pie** Benjamin Moore Cupid's Dart 1385; Sherwin-Williams 7577 Blackberry **5 Ansonia Peach** Benjamin Moore Ansonia Peach HC-52; Sherwin-Williams 6655 Adventure Orange **6 Titanium White** Benjamin Moore Distant Gray OC-68; Sherwin-Williams 6995 Superwhite

PAGE 101 GRAY SKIES
1 Harlequin Blue Benjamin Moore Harlequin Blue 830; Sherwin-Williams 6235 Foggy Day **2 Blue-Gray** Benjamin Moore Lake Placid 827; Sherwin-Williams 6225 Sleepy Blue **3 Graphite** Benjamin Moore Rock Gray 1615;Sherwin-Williams 7674 Peppercorn **4 Cord** Farrow & Ball Cord 16; Sherwin-Williams 7159 Gourd **5 Blueberry** Benjamin Moore Grappa 1393; Farrow & Ball Pelt 254 **6 Violet Petal** Benjamin Moore Violet Petal 1382; Sherwin-Williams 6017 Intuitive

PAGE 101 COOL CUISINE
1 Military Uniform Benjamin Moore Stratford Blue 831; Sherwin-Williams 6251 Outerspace **2 Gustavian Gray** Benjamin Moore Manor Blue 1627; Sherwin-Williams 6256 Serious Gray **3 Pueblo** Benjamin Moore Georgia Pink 2092-60; Sherwin-Williams 6031 Glamour **4 Mother of Pearl** Benjamin Moore Swiss Coffee OC-45; Paint & Paper Library Sand I **5 Pitch Blue** Farrow & Ball Pitch Blue 220; Sherwin-Williams 6230 Rainstorm **6 Summer Sunshine** Benjamin Moore American Cheese 2019-40; Farrow & Ball Print Room Yellow 69

AVOCADO & PISTACHIO

PAGE 105
Apple Lime Benjamin Moore Apple Lime Cocktail 420; Sherwin-Williams 6923 Festival Green **Forest Hills Green** Benjamin Moore Forest Hills Green 433; Sherwin-Williams 6432 Garden Spot **Mint Tea** Benjamin Moore Scenic View 424; Sherwin-Williams 6731 Picnic **Faded Green** Benjamin Moore Palisades Park 439; Sherwin-Williams 7167 Ornamental Kale **Sage Green** Benjamin Moore Kittery Point Green HC-119; Sherwin-Williams 6178 Clary Sage 7167 Ornamental Kale **Chameleon** Benjamin Moore St. John's Bay 584; Sherwin-Williams 6745 Lark Green

PAGE 108 CELERY
1 Springhill Green Benjamin Moore Springhill Green 412; Sherwin-Williams 6922 Outrageous Green **2 Lime Twist** Benjamin Moore Lime Twist 425; Sherwin-Williams 6930 Laudable Lime **3 Mint Tea** Benjamin Moore Scenic View 424; Sherwin-Williams 6731 Picnic **4 Pine Sprigs** Benjamin Moore Pine Sprigs 423; Sherwin-Williams 6709 Gleeful **5 Chrome Green** Benjamin Moore New Retro 422; Sherwin-Williams 6716 Dancing Green **6 Pale Pear** Benjamin Moore Green Cove Springs 421; Sherwin-Williams G928 Green Vibes **7 Gustavian Green** Harrisburg Green HC-132; Sherwin-Williams 6180 Oakmoss **8 Spring Greens** Benjamin Moore Sherwood Green HC-118; Sherwin-Williams 2826 Colonial Revival Green Stone **9 Sage Green** Benjamin Moore Kittery Point Green HC-119; Sherwin-Williams 6178 Clary Sage **10 Pine Tree** Benjamin Moore Guilford Green HC-116; Farrow & Ball Cooking Apple Green 32 **11 Mint Chocolate Chip** Benjamin Moore Mint Chocolate Chip 436; Sherwin-Williams 6429 Baize Green **12 Chicory Tip** Benjamin Moore Van Alen Green HC-120; Sherwin-Williams 6722 Cucumber

PAGE 109 APPLE
1 Apple Lime Benjamin Moore Apple Lime Cocktail 420; Sherwin-Williams 6923 Festival Green **2 Apple Orchard** Benjamin Moore Malachy Green 419; Sherwin-Williams 6922 Outrageous Green **3 Lime Grass** Benjamin Moore Willow Springs Green 418; Sherwin-Williams 6920 Centre Stage **4 Bramley** Benjamin Moore Feel the Energy 417; Sherwin-Williams 6717 Lime Rickey **5 Tasty Apple** Benjamin Moore Tasty Apple 416; Sherwin-Williams 6710 Melange Green **6 Green Sherbet** Benjamin Moore Riverdale Green 415; Sherwin-Williams 6709 Gleeful **7 Emerald** Benjamin Moore Scotch Plains Green 587; Sherwin-Williams 6927 Greenbelt **8 Jade** Benjamin Moore Northern Lights 586; Farrow & Ball Arsenic 214 **9 Mint Julep** Benjamin Moore Lady Liberty 585; Sherwin-Williams 6934 Rally Green **10 Chameleon** Benjamin Moore St. John's Bay 584; Sherwin-Williams 6745 Lark Green **11 Celadon** Benjamin Moore Mountainview 583; Sherwin-Williams 6932 Spirited Green **12 Cool Mint** Benjamin Moore Cool Mint 582; Sherwin-Williams 6736 Jocular Green

PAGE 109 OLIVE
1 Antique Green Benjamin Moore Alligator Alley 441; Sherwin-Williams 6181 Secret Garden **2 Herb Garden** Benjamin Moore Herb Garden 434,Sherwin-Williams 6433 Inverness **3 Forest Hills Green** Benjamin Moore Forest Hills Green 433; Sherwin-Williams 6432 Garden Spot **4 Faded Green** Benjamin Moore Palisades Park 439; Sherwin-Williams 7167 Ornamental Kale **5 Spring Valley** Benjamin Moore Spring Valley 438; SherwinWilliams 6186 Dried Thyme **6 Fresh Dew** Benjamin Moore Fresh Dew 435; Sherwin-Williams 6436 Bonsai Thrift **7 Deep Sea Green** Benjamin Moore Crisp Romaine 686; Sherwin-Williams 0065 Vogue Green **8 Gothic Green** Benjamin Moore Gothic Green 637; Sherwin-Williams 6440 Courtyard **9 Willow Grove** Benjamin Moore Willow Grove 636; Sherwin-Williams 6460 Kale Green **10 Winchester Sage** Benjamin Moore Winchester Sage 628; Sherwin-Williams 6459 Judite **11 Meadow** Benjamin Moore Spring Break 627; Sherwin-Williams 6444 Inland **12 Dew** Benjamin Moore Feather Green 625; Sherwin-Williams 6736 Jocular Green

PAGE 112 FOREST SYMPHONY
1 Sage Green Benjamin Moore Kittery Point Green HC-119 **2 Chicory Tip** Benjamin Moore Van Alen Green HC-120 **3 White Truffle** Benjamin Moore Powder Sand OC -113; Sherwin-Williams 0051 Classic Ivory **4 Vienna Green** Benjamin Moore Vienna Green 538; Sherwin-Williams 6720 Pardise **5 Caribbean Coast** Benjamin Moore Caribbean Coast 2065-60; Sherwin-Williams 6953 Candid Blue **6 Saffron** Benjamin Moore Jack o'Lantern 2156-30; Sherwin-Williams 6643 Yam

PAGE 112 GUSTAVIAN GREEN
1 Mint Chocolate Chip Benjamin Moore Mint Choc Chip 436; Sherwin-Williams 6429 Baize Green **2 Gustavian Green** Benjamin Moore Harrisburg Green HC-132; Sherwin-Williams 6180 Oak-moss **3 Dark Oak** Benjamin Moore Fox Run 1229; Sherwin-Williams 6110 Steady Brown **4 Deep Night Blue** Benjamin Moore Drawing Room Blue 253; Sherwin-Williams 6237 Dark Night **5 Cook's Blue** Farrow & Ball Cook's Blue 237; Sherwin-Williams 6516 Down Pour **6 Clotted Cream** Benjamin Moore Timid White OC-39; Sherwin-Williams 6421 Celery

PAGE 113 FRIED GREEN TOMATOES
1 Sage Green Benjamin Moore Kittery Point Green HC-119; Sherwin-Williams 6178 Clary Sage **2 Spring Greens** Benjamin Moore Sherwood Green HC-118; Sherwin-Williams 2826 Colonial Revival Green Stone **3 Pelican Gray** Benjamin Moore Pelican Gray 1612; Sherwin-Williams 6254 Lazy Gray **4 Mother of Pearl** Benjamin Moore Swiss Coffee OC-45; Paint & Paper Library Sand I **5 Ruby Red** Benjamin Moore Ruby Red 2001-10 Sherwin-Williams 6869 Stop **6 Full Bloom** Benjamin Moore Full Bloom 2001-50; Sherwin-Williams 6591 Amaryllis

PAGE 116 SAGE HAVEN
1 Mint Julep Benjamin Moore Lady Liberty 585; Sherwin-Williams 6934 Rally Green **2 Emerald** Benjamin Moore Scotch Plains Green 587; Sherwin-Williams 6927 Greenbelt **3 String** Farrow & Ball String 8; Sherwin-Williams 0036 Buckram Binding **4 Dark Beige** Farrow & Ball Cat's Paw 240; Sherwin-Williams 6109 Hopsack **5 Blazer Red** Farrow & Ball Blazer 212; Sherwin-Williams 7582 Salute **6 Fashion Pink** Benjamin Moore Fashion Pink 2009-50; Sherwin-Williams 6591 Amaryllis

PAGE 117 APPLE DINER
1 Bramley Benjamin Moore Feel the Energy 417; Sherwin-Williams 6717 Lime Rickey **2 Midnight Green** Farrow & Ball Munster Green 224 **3 Paddington Blue** Benjamin Moore Paddington Blue 791; Sherwin-Williams 6966 Blueblood **4 Blue Bayou** Benjamin Moore Blue Bayou 801; Sherwin-Williams 6501 Manitou Blue **5 Natural White** Farrow & Ball Strong White 2001; Sherwin-Williams 7596 Only Natural **6 Seed Pod** Farrow & Ball Savage Ground 213; Sherwin-Williams 7179 Sunflower Seed

Page 120 GREEN MIST
1 Faded Green Benjamin Moore Palisades Park 439; Sherwin-Williams 7167 Ornamental Kale **2 Pine Tree** Benjamin Moore Guildford Green HC-116; Farrow & Ball Cooking Apple Green 32 **3 Cornforth White** Farrow & Ball Cornforth White; Francesca's Paints The MIST **4 Beige Sand** Benjamin Moore Shabby Chic 1018; Sherwin-Williams 7712 Townhouse Tan **5 Brassy Gold** Benjamin Moore Blair Gold HC-22; Sherwin-Williams 6405 Fervent Brass **6 London Burgundy** Benjamin Moore New London Burgundy HC-61; Sherwin-Williams 7630 Raisin

121 CHINESE GREEN
1 Deep Sea Green Benjamin Moore Crisp Romaine 686; Sherwin-Williams 0065 Vogue Green **2 All White** Farrow & Ball All White 2005; Paint & Paper Library Chaste **3 Willow Grove** Benjamin Moore Willow Grove 636; Sherwin-Williams 6460 Kale Green **4 Miami Teal** Benjamin Moore Miami Teal 656; Sherwin-Williams 6746 Julep **5 Dinky Pink** Farrow & Ball Middleton Pink 245; Paint & Paper Library Coral 1 **6 Claret Rose** Benjamin Moore Claret Rose 2008-20; Paint & Paper Library Beetlenut

PAGE 121 MOROCCAN MIX
1 Forest Hills Green Benjamin Moore Forest Hills Green 433; Sherwin-Williams 6432 Garden Spot **2 Strong Red** Benjamin Moore Poppy 1315; Sherwin-Williams 6863 Lusty Red **3 Summer Straw** Fine Paints of Europe LP22; Paint & Paper Library Straw IV **4 Great Green** Fine Paints of Europe SK 19; Sherwin-Williams 6430 Great Green **5 Pulsating Blue** Benjamin Moore Rocky Mountain Sky 2066-40; Sherwin-Williams 6964 Pul-sating Blue **6 Buttercup Yellow** Fine Paints of Europe CG4; Sherwin-Williams 2858 Harvest Gold

EARTH & CLAY

PAGE 125
Mud Flat Benjamin Moore Acorn Yellow 2161-40; Sherwin-Williams 6361 Autumnal **Brown Sugar** Benjamin Moore Maple Sugar 2160-30; Farrow & Ball Sand 45 **Mocha Express** Benjamin Moore Whitall Brown HC-69; Sherwin-Williams 7055 Enduring Bronze **Texas Rose** Benjamin Moore Texas Rose 2092-40; Farrow & Ball Porphry Pink 49 **Beige Sand** Benjamin Moore Shabby Chic 1018; Sherwin-Williams 7712 Townhouse Tan **Sable Fur** Benjamin Moore Dellwood Sand 1019; Sherwin-Williams 6046 Swing Brown **Cracked Wheat** Benjamin Moore Jamesboro Gold HC-88; Sherwin-Williams 6103 Tea Chest **Milk Chocolate** Benjamin Moore Antique Copper 1169; Sherwin-Williams 2803 Rookwood Terra Cotta

PAGE 128 CINNAMON
1 Santa Fe Benjamin Moore Peanut Butter 2159-20; Sherwin-Williams 6657 Amber Wave **2 Allspice** Benjamin Moore Caramel Corn 2160-10; Sherwin-Williams 6370 Saucy Gold **3 Brown Sugar** Benjamin Moore Maple Sugar 2160-30; Farrow & Ball Sand 45 **4 Mud Flat** Benjamin Moore Acorn Yellow 2161-40; Sherwin-Williams 6361 Autumnal **5 Ocher** Benjamin Moore Roasted Sesame Seed 2160-40; Sherwin-Williams 6360 Folksy Gold **6 Oklahoma Wheat** Benjamin Moore Oklahoma Wheat 2160-50; Paint & Paper Library Whitington **7 Burnt Sienna** Benjamin Moore Dried Mustard 2158-10; Sherwin-Williams 6355 Truepenny **8 Orange Tan** Benjamin Moore Autumn Orange 2156-10; Paint & Paper Library The Long Room **9 Saffron** Benjamin Moore Jack O'Lantern 2156-30; Sherwin-Williams 6643 Yam **10 Beeswax** Benjamin Moore Beeswax 2157-40; Sherwin-Williams 6633 Inventive Orange **11 Acorn** Benjamin Moore August Morning 2156-40; Sherwin-Williams 6649 Tango **12 Ashbury Sand** Benjamin Moore Asbury Sand 2156-50; Sherwin-Williams 6647 Exciting Orange

PAGE 128 ADOBE
1 Milk Chocolate Benjamin Moore Antique Copper 1169; Sherwin-Williams 2803 Rookwood Terra Cotta **2 Noisette** Benjamin Moore Wildnerness Cabin 1168; Sherwin-Williams 0007 Decorous Amber **3 Mink** Benjamin Moore Fox Hedge Tan 1167; Sherwin-Williams 2804 Renwick Rose Beige **4 Putty** Benjamin Moore Groundhog Day 1166; Sherwin-Williams 0039 Portrait Tone **5 Milk Shake** Benjamin Moore Milk Shake 1165; Sherwin-Williams 0069 Rose Tan **6 Pumice** Benjamin Moore Pink Coastal Cottage 1164; Paint & Paper Library Coral II **7 Oxblood** Benjamin Moore Sienna 2092-20; Sherwin-Williams 2839 Roycroft Copper Red **8 Boston Brick** Benjamin Moore Boston Brick 2092-30; Sherwin-Williams 2838 Polished Mahogany **9 Texas Rose** Benjamin Moore Texas Rose 2092-40; Farrow & Ball Porphry Pink 49 **10 Polished Plaster** Benjamin Moore Titanic Rose 2092-50; Sherwin-Williams 6053 Reddened Red **11 Pueblo** Benjamin Moore Georgia Pink 2092-60; Sherwin-Williams 6304 Pressed Flower **12 Fairest Pink** Benjamin Moore Fairest Pink 2092-70; Sherwin-Williams 6872 Gaiety

PAGE 129 MOLE
1 Taupetone Benjamin Moore Taupetone 1013; Sherwin-Williams 6068 Brevity Brown **2 Woodacres** Benjamin Moore Woodacres 1020; Sherwin-Williams 2836 Quartersawn Oak **3 Sable Fur** Benjamin Moore Dellwood Sand 1019; Sherwin-Williams 6046 Swing Brow **4 Tupelo Taupe** Benjamin Moore Whispering Woods 1012; Sherwin-Williams 6067 Mocha **5 Beige Sand** Benjamin Moore Shabby Chic 1018; Sherwin-Williams 7712 Townhouse Tan **6 Chalk Pit** Benjamin Moore Litchfield Gray HC-78; Sherwin-Williams 7723 Colony Buff **7 Brownstone** Benjamin Moore Woodcliff Lake 980; Sherwin-Williams 6041 Otter **8 Café Crème** Stampede 979; Sherwin-Williams 7027 Well-Bred Brown **9 Raccoon Hollow** Benjamin Moore Raccoon Hollow 978; Sherwin-Williams 7545 Pier **10 Brandon Beige** Benjamin Moore Brandon Beige 977; Sherwin-Williams 2855 Sycamore Tan **11 French Linen** Benjamin Moore Coastal Fog 976; Sherwin-Williams 7716 Croissant **12 Tapestry Beige** Benjamin Moore Tapestry Beige 975; Sherwin-Williams 0036 Buckram Binding

PAGE 129 CHOCOLATE
1 Cup O'Java Benjamin Moore Cup O'Java 1246; Sherwin-Williams 6006 Black Bean **2 Saddle Brown** Benjamin Moore Saddle Brown 2164-10; Sherwin-Williams 6048 Terra Brun **3 Savannah** Benjamin Moore Rich Clay Brown 2164-30; **4 Bitter Chocolate** Benjamin Moore Coyote Trail 1224; Sherwin-Williams 6062 Rugged Brown **5 Dark Oak** Benjamin Moore Fox Run 1229; Sherwin-Williams 6110 Steady Brown **6 Nutmeg** Benjamin Moore Nutmeg 1227; Sherwin-Williams 7701 Cavern Clay **7 Mahogany** Benjamin Moore Topeka Taupe 1463; Sherwin-Williams 6076 Turkish Coffee **8 Mocha Express** Benjamin Moore Whitall Brown HC-69; Sherwin-Williams 7055 Enduring Bronze **9 Truffle** Benjamin Moore Long Valley Birch 1021; Sherwin-Williams 6104 Kaffee **10 Cracked Wheat** Benjamin Moore Jamesboro Gold HC-88; Sherwin-Williams 6103 Tea Chest **11 Smooth Pebble** Benjamin Moore Alexandria Beige HC-77; Sherwin-Williams 6082 Cobble Brown **12 Camel's Back** Benjamin Moore Manchester Tan HC-81; Sherwin-Williams 6143 Basket Beige

PAGE 132 ISLAND SPICE
1 Brown Sugar Benjamin Moore Maple Sugar 2160-30; Farrow & Ball Sand 45 **2 Beige Sand** Benjamin Moore Shabby Chic 1018; Sherwin-Williams 7712 Townhouse Tan **3 Golden Yellow** Fine Paints of Europe CG4; Sherwin-Williams 6899 Nasturtium **4 Mandarin Fruit** Benjamin Moore Fruit Punch 140; Sherwin-Williams 6882 Daredevil **5 Gray Suede** Farrow & Ball Charleston Gray 243; Sherwin-Williams 6082 Cobble Brown **6 Leather** Benjamin Moore Terra Mauve 105; Sherwin-Williams 7175 Curly Willow

PAGE 133 FEELING THE HEAT
1 Acorn Benjamin Moore August Morning 2156-40; Sherwin Williams 6649 Tango **2 Orange Tan** Benjamin Moore Autumn Orange 2156-10; Paint & Paper Library The Long Room **3 Clover White** Benjamin Moore Ambrosia 893; Sherwin-Williams 6323 Romance **4 Red Rock** Benjamin Moore Red Rock 2005-10; Sherwin-Williams Cherry Tomato 6864 **5 Chili Pepper** Benjamin Moore Tricycle Red 2000-20; Sherwin-Williams 6866 Hearttthro **6 Jet Night** Benjamin Moore Black Bean Soup 2130-10; Sherwin-Williams 6991 Black Magic

PAGE 133 BATHED IN SPICE
1 Texas Rose Benjamin Moore Texas Rose 2092-40; Farrow & Ball Porphry Pink 49 **2 Tapestry Beige** Benjamin Moore Tapestry Beige 975; Sherwin-Williams 0036 Buckram Binding **3 Cotton Ball** Benjamin Moore Horizon OC-53: Farrow & Ball Blackened 2011 **4**

Meadowlands Green Benjamin Moore Meadowlands Green 2036-40; Sherwin-Williams 6746 Julep **5 Racing Green** Benjamin Moore Cat's Eye 2036-10; Sherwin-Williams 6461 Isle of Pines **6 Olympus Green** Benjamin Moore Olympus Green 679; Sherwin-Williams 2847 Roycroft Bottle Green

PAGE 136 TREETOP COOL
1 Noisette Benjamin Moore Wildnerness Cabin 1168; Sherwin-Williams 0007 Decorous Amber **2 Putty** Benjamin Moore Groundhog Day 1166; Sherwin-Williams 0039 Portrait Tone **3 Willow Grove** Benjamin Moore Willow Grove 636; Sherwin-Williams 6460 Kale Green **4 Orbit Glow** Benjamin Moore Jupiter Glow 021; Sherwin-Williams 6883 Raucous Orange **5 Hot Red** Benjamin Moore Smoldering Red 2007-10; Sherwin-Williams 6328 Fireweed **6 Vineyard** Benjamin Moore Vintage Wine 2116-20; Sherwin-Williams 6279 Black Swan

PAGE 137 MUD, GLORIOUS MUD
1 Milk Chocolate Benjamin Moore Antique Copper 1169; Sherwin-Williams 2803 Rookwood Terra Cotta **2 Pumice** Benjamin Moore Pink Coastal Cottage 1164; Paint & Paper Library Coral II **3 All White** Farrow & Ball All White 2005; Fine Paints of Europe Sk-14 **4 Hadley Red** Benjamin Moore Hadley Red HC-65; Sherwin-Williams 7150 Vineyard **5 Monticello Rose** Benjamin Moore Monticello Rose HC-63; Sherwin-Williams 6032 Dutch Cocoa **6 Toasted Bean** Benjamin Moore Van Buren Brown HC-70; Sherwin-Williams 6006 Black Bean

PAGE 140 SILVER GRAY
1 Tupelo Taupe Benjamin Moore Whispering Woods 1012; Sherwin-Williams 6067 Mocha **2 Shadow Gray** Benjamin Moore Shadow Gray 2125-40; Sherwin-Williams 7046 Anonymous **3 Cloudy Gray** Benjamin Moore Cloudy Gray 2107-70; Sherwin-Williams 7553 Fragile Beauty **4 Cotton Ball** Benjamin Moore Horizon OC-53: Farrow & Ball Blackened 2011 **5 Grass** Sherwin-Williams 6923 Festival Green; Benjamin Moore Rosemary Green 2029-30 **6 Jungle** Sherwin-Williams 2809 Rookwood Shutter Green; Fine Paints of Europe SK-36

PAGE 141 FIRED EARTH
1 Sable Fur Benjamin Moore Dellwood Sand 1019; Sherwin-Williams 6046 Swing Brown **2 Flax** Benjamin Moore Flax 2098-50; Sherwin-Williams 7525 Tree Branch **3 Savory Cream** Benjamin Moore Savory Cream 2105-70; Sherwin-Williams 6093 Familiar Beige **4 Pumpkin Spice** Benjamin Moore Pumpkin Spice 126; Sherwin-Williams 6642 Rhumba Orange **5 Shy Cherry** Benjamin Moore Shy Cherry 2007-20; Sherwin-Williams 6608 Rave Red **6 Misty Morning** Benjamin Moore Violet Mist 1437; Sherwin-Williams 7646 First Star

PAGE 144 TOPAZ & TOFFEE
1 Mahogany Benjamin Moore Topeka Taupe 1463; Sherwin-Williams 6076 Turkish Coffee **2 Salsa** Benjamin Moore Salsa 2009-20; Sherwin-Williams 6601 Tanager **3 Café Latte** Benjamin Moore Ocean Beach 958; Sherwin-Williams 0010 Wickerwork **4 Glimmer** Benjamin Moore Glimmer 42; Sherwin-Williams 6685 Trinket **5 Citronee** Benjamin Moore Citronee 281; Sherwin-Williams 6896 Solé **6 Seaport Blue** Benjamin Moore Color Preview Seaport Blue 2060 30; Sherwin-Williams 6966 Blueblood

PAGE 145 MOCHA LIVING
1 Cup O'Java Benjamin Moore Cup O'Java 1246; Sherwin-Williams 6006 Black Bean **2 Saddle Brown** Benjamin Moore Saddle Brown 2164-10; Sherwin-Williams 6048 Terra Brun **3 Forest Green** Farrow & Ball Calke Green 34; Sherwin-Williams 6461 Isle of Pines **4 Antique Brown** Farrow & Ball Buff 20; Sherwin-Williams 0045 Antiquarian Brown **5 Deep Gilt** Benjamin Moore Goldenhurst 196; Sherwin-Williams 6370 Saucy Gold **6 Mouse Gray** Benjamin Moore San Antonio Gray AC-29; Sherwin-Williams 7080 Quest Gray

NIGHT & DAY

PAGE 149
Stainless Steel Benjamin Moore Blue Lace 1625; Sherwin-Williams 6204 Sea Salt **Snow White** Benjamin Moore Snow White OC-66; Sherwin-Williams 7566 Westhighland White **Pewter** Benjamin Moore Silent Night 1613; Sherwin-Williams 7655 Stamped Concrete **Blackboard** Benjamin Moore Ocean Floor 1630; Sherwin-Williams 6993 Black of Night **Airforce Blue** Benjamin Moore Kitty Gray 1589; Sherwin-Williams 6216 Jasper **White Ice** Benjamin Moore White Ice OC-58; Sherwin-Williams 7102 White Flour

PAGE 152 SNOW
1 Nautical White Benjamin Moore Misty Air OC-44; Sherwin-Williams 6157 Favorite Tan **2 Arctic Fox** Benjamin Moore French Canvas OC-41; Paint & Paper Library Marble I **3 China Cup** Benjamin Moore Old Prairie OC-42; Sherwin-Williams 6156 Ramie **4 Egyptian Cotton** Benjamin Moore Overcast OC-43; Paint & Paper Library Sand III **5 Chalk** Benjamin Moore Halo OC-46; Sherwin-Williams 0011 Crewel Tan **6 Mother of Pearl** Benjamin Moore Swiss Coffee OC-45; Paint & Paper Library Sand I **7 White Ice** Benjamin Moore White Ice OC-58; Sherwin-Williams 7102 White Flour **8 Polar Bear** Benjamin Moore White Diamond OC-61; Sherwin-Williams 6427 Sprout **9 Tundra Ice** Benjamin Moore Baby's Breath OC-62; Sherwin-Williams 7551 Greek Villa **10 Winter Snow** Benjamin Moore Winter Snow OC-63; Sherwin-Williams 7005 Pure White **11 Titanium White** Benjamin Moore Distant Gray OC-68; Sherwin-Williams 6995 Superwhite **12 Snow White** Benjamin Moore Snow White OC-66; Sherwin-Williams 7566 Westhighland White

PAGE 152 METALLIC GRAY
1 Gray Mountain Benjamin Moore Gray Mountain 1462; Sherwin-Williams 7675 Sealskin **2 Sterling Silver** Benjamin Moore Sterling Silver 1461; Sherwin-Williams 7019 Gauntlet Gray **3 Dove** Benjamin Moore Silver Dollar 1460; Sherwin-Williams 6074 Spalding Gray **4 Pearl** Benjamin Moore Metro Gray 1459; Sherwin-Williams 7045 Intellectual Gray **5 Silver Birch** Benjamin Moore Silver Bells 1458; Sherwin-Williams 2844 Roycroft Mist Gray **6 Chrome** Benjamin Moore White Winged Dove 1457; Sherwin-Williams 7531 Canvas Tan **7 Blackboard** Benjamin Moore Ocean Floor 1630; Sherwin-Williams 6993 Black of Night **8 Bachelor Blue** Benjamin Moore Bachelor Blue 1629; Sherwin-Williams 7605 Gale Force **9 Black Ash** Benjamin Moore Comet 1628; Sherwin-Williams 6250 Granite Peak **10 Gustavian Gray** Benjamin Moore Manor Blue 1627; Sherwin-Williams 6256 Serious Gray **11 Gunmetal** Benjamin Moore Gentle Gray 1626; Sherwin-Williams 6255 Morning Fog **12 Stainless Steel** Benjamin Moore Blue Lace 1625; Sherwin-Williams 6204 Sea Salt

PAGE 153 SLATE
1 Charcoal Benjamin Moore Cheating Heart 1617; Sherwin-Williams 6258 Tricorn Black **2 Deep Slate** Benjamin Moore Stormy Sky 1616; Sherwin-Williams 7069 Iron Ore **3 Graphite** Benjamin Moore Rock Gray 1615;Sherwin-Williams 7674 Peppercorn **4 Elephant Gray** Benjamin Moore Delray Gray 1614; Sherwin-Williams 7669 Summit Gray **5 Pewter** Benjamin Moore Silent Night 1613; Sherwin-Williams 7655 Stamped Concrete **6 Pelican Gray** Benjamin Moore Pelican Gray 1612; Sherwin-Williams 6254 Lazy Gray **7 Squid Ink** Benjamin Moore Midnight Blue 1638; Sherwin-Williams 6994 Greenblack **8 Airforce Blue** Benjamin Moore Kitty Gray 1589; Sherwin-Williams 6216 Jasper **9 Bluff Cove** Benjamin Moore Gibraltar Cliffs 1587; Sherwin-Williams 7750 Olympic Range **10 Silver Mink** Benjamin Moore Silver Mink 1587; Sherwin-Williams 6249 Storm Cloud **11 Ice Blue** Benjamin Moore Brittany Blue 1633; Sherwin-Williams 6248 Jubilee **12 Gray Ash** Benjamin Moore Glass Slipper 1632; Sherwin-Williams 6254 Lazy Gray

PAGE 156 LOFTY WHITES
1 Jute Benjamin Moore Winds Breath OC-24; Sherwin-Williams 7100 Arcade White **2 Charcoal** Benjamin Moore Cheating Heart 1617; Sherwin-Williams 6258 Tricorn Black **3 Forest Hills Green** Benjamin Moore Forest Hills Green 433; Sherwin-Williams 6432 Garden Spot **4 Turkish Coffee** Fine Paints of Europe Sk35; Sherwin-Williams 6076 Turkish Coffee **5 Bronzed Brown** Farrow & Ball Dauphin 54; Sherwin-Williams 7034 Status Bronze **6 Walled Garden** Benjamin Moore Avon Green HC-126; Sherwin-Williams 6181 Secret Garden

PAGE 157 WHITE WOOD
1 Mother of Pearl Benjamin Moore Swiss Coffee OC-45; Paint & Paper Library Sand I **2 Pale Pear** Benjamin Moore Green Cove Springs 421; Sherwin-Williams G928 Green Vibes **3 Yukon Sky** Benjamin Moore Yukon Sky 1439; Francesca's Paints The MARSH **4 Tupelo Green** Benjamin Moore Aberdeen Green 631; Sherwin-Williams 6730 Romaine **5 Cayman Blue** Benjamin Moore Cayman Blue 2060-50; Sherwin-Williams 6788 Capri **6 Passion Plum** Benjamin Moore Passion Plum 2073-30; Sherwin-Williams 0072 Deep Maroon

PAGE 161 DECO SHIMMER
1 Dove Benjamin Moore Silver Dollar 1460; Sherwin-Williams 6074 Spalding Gray **2 Bluff Cove** Benjamin Moore Gibraltar Cliffs 1587; Sherwin-Williams 7750 Olympic Range **3 Dark Walnut** Benjamin Moore Dark Walnut 1358; Sherwin-Williams 7083 Darkroom **4 Velvety Red** Benjamin Moore Crushed Velvet 2076-10; Sherwin-Williams 6307 Fine Wine **5 Green Horizon** Benjamin Moore Harbor Haze 2136-60; Sherwin-Williams 6744 Reclining Green **6 Green Hint** Benjamin Moore Green Tint 2139-60; Sherwin-Williams 6728 White Willow

PAGE 161 PEWTER PERFECTION
1 Gustavian Gray Benjamin Moore Manor Blue 1627; Sherwin-Williams 6256 Serious Gray **2 Stainless Steel** Benjamin Moore Blue Lace 1625; Sherwin-Williams 6204 Sea Salt **3 Darkest Grape** Benjamin Moore Darkest Grape 2069-30; Francesca's Paints The STORM **4 Antique Lace** Benjamin Moore Antique Lace 922; Sherwin-Williams 7159 Gourd **5 Natural Canvas** Benjamin Moore Silver Satin OC-26; Fine Paints of Europe JL2 **6 Smoky Blue** Benjamin Moore Airway 828; Sherwin-Williams 7604 Smoky Blue

PAGE 164 TROPICAL GLAMOUR
1 Graphite Benjamin Moore Rock Gray 1615;Sherwin-Williams 7674 Peppercorn **2 Pelican Gray** Benjamin Moore Pelican Gray 1612; Sherwin-Williams 6254 Lazy Gray **3 Cotton Ball** Benjamin Moore Horizon OC-53; : Farrow & Ball Blackened 2011 **4 Cabernet** Benjamin Moore Cabernet 2116-30; Sherwin-Williams 6272 Plum Brown **5 Witching Hour** Benjamin Moore Witching Hour 2120-30; Sherwin-Williams 6990 Caviar **6 Province Blue** Benjamin Moore Province Blue 2135-40; Shserwin-Williams 7604 Smoky Blue

PAGE 164 BLACK NOTES
1 Pelican Gray Benjamin Moore Pelican Gray 1612; Sherwin-Williams 6254 Lazy Gray **2 Silver Mink** Benjamin Moore Silver Mink 1587; Sherwin-Williams 6249 Storm Cloud **3 Chrome** Benjamin Moore White Winged Dove 1457; Sherwin-Williams 7531 Canvas Tan **4 Marble Canyon** Benjamin Moore Marble Canyon 227; Sherwin-Williams 2384 Birdseye Maple **5 Potters Clay** Benjamin Moore Potters Clay 1221; Sherwin-Williams 7709 Copper Pot **6 Deep Indigo** Benjamin Moore Deep Indigo 1442; Sherwin-Williams 6188 Shade-Grown

PAGE 165 FINE DINING
1 Charcoal Benjamin Moore Cheating Heart 1617; Sherwin-Williams 6258 Tricorn Black **2 Lantern Light** Fine Paints of Europe SK 25; Sherwin-Williams 6687 Lantern Light **3 Clotted Cream** Benjamin Moore Timid White OC-39; Sherwin-Williams 6421 Celery **4 Newburg Green** Benjamin Moore Newburg Green HC-158; Sherwin-Williams 6230 Rainstorm **5 Hollow Brown** Benjamin Moore Fox Hollow Brown 1235; Sherwin-Williams 7177 Root Beer Float **6 Sag Harbor Gray** Benjamin Moore Sag Harbor Gray HC-95; Sherwin-Williams 7733 Bamboo Shoot

Page 166 NORTHERN LIGHTS
1 Airforce Blue Benjamin Moore Kitty Gray 1589; Sherwin-Williams 6216 Jasper **2 Pewter** Benjamin Moore Silent Night 1613; Sherwin-Williams 7655 Stamped Concrete **3 Titanium White** Benjamin Moore Distant Gray OC-68; Sherwin-Williams 6995 Superwhite **4 Georgian Green** Benjamin Moore Georgian Green HC-115; Sherwin-Williams 2826 Colonial Revival Green Stone **5 Richmond Gold** Benjamin Moore Richmond Gold HC-41; Sherwin-Williams 6118 Leather Bound **6 Smooth Pebble** Benjamin Moore Alexandria Beige HC-77; Sherwin-Williams 6082 Cobble Brown

PAGE 166 ENTIRELY TAR
1 Charcoal Benjamin Moore Cheating Heart 1617; Sherwin-Williams 6258 Tricorn Black **2 White Ice** Benjamin Moore White Ice OC-58; Sherwin-Williams 7102 White Flour **3 Elephant Gray** Benjamin Moore Delray Gray 1614; Sherwin-Williams 7669 Summit Gray **4 Midnight Navy** Benjamin Moore Hale Navy HC-154; Sherwin-Williams 6993 Black of Night **5 Dove** Benjamin Moore Silver Dollar 1460; Sherwin-Williams 6074 Spalding Gray **6 Gray Shingle** Sherwin-Williams 7670 Gray Shingle; Farrow & Ball Hardwick White 5

PAGE 167 GREEN & BLACK
1 Charcoal Benjamin Moore Cheating Heart 1617; Sherwin-Williams 6258 Tricorn Black **2 Pelican Gray** Benjamin Moore Pelican Gray 1612; Sherwin-Williams 6254 Lazy Gray **3 Snow White** Benjamin Moore Snow White OC-66; Sherwin-Williams 7566 Westhighland White **4 Fairmont Green** Benjamin Moore Fairmont Green HC-127; Sherwin-Williams 6453 Cilantro **5 Salisbury Green** Benjamin Moore Salisbury Green HC-139; Sherwin-Williams 6192 Coastal Plain **6 Bright and Early** Benjamin Moore Bright and Early 834; Sherwin-Williams 6770 Bubble

PAGE 167 SAFARI PLAINS
1 Airforce Blue Benjamin Moore Kitty Gray 1589; Sherwin-Williams 6216 Jasper **2 Ocher** Benjamin Moore Roasted Sesame Seed 2160-40; Sherwin-Williams 6360 Folksy Gold **3 Mother of Pearl** Benjamin Moore Swiss Coffee OC-45; Paint & Paper Library Sand I **4 Galveston Gray** Benjamin Moore Galveston Gray AC-27; Sherwin-Williams 6278 **5 Roxbury Caramel** Benjamin Moore Roxbury Caramel HC-42; Sherwin-Williams 6377 Butterscotch **6 Shaker Beige** Benjamin Moore Shaker Beige HC-45; Sherwin-Williams 6128 Blonde

PANNACOTTA & CAPPUCCINO

PAGE 171
Alabaster Benjamin Moore White Ice OC-58; Francesca's Paints Pavilion **Natural Canvas** Benjamin Moore Silver Satin OC-26; Fine Paints of Europe JL2 **Butter Churn** Benjamin Moore Opal 891; Fine Paints of Europe SK-2 **Café Latte** Benjamin Moore Ocean Beach 958; Sherwin-Williams 0010 Wickerwork **Lily of the Valley** Benjamin Moore Lily of the Valley 905; Francesca's Paints Sand I **Bleached Beech** Benjamin Moore Palace White 956; Francesca's Paints Moonlight

PAGE 174 RICOTTA
1 Cotton Ball Benjamin Moore Horizon OC-53: Farrow & Ball Blackened 2011 **2 Orchid** Benjamin Moore November Rain OC-50; Francesca's Paints Truffle **3 Clotted Cream** Benjamin Moore Timid White OC-39; Sherwin-Williams 6421 Celery **4 Mother of Pearl** Benjamin Moore Swiss Coffee OC-45; Paint & Paper Library Sand I **5 Alabaster** Benjamin Moore White Ice OC-58; Francesca's Paints Pavilion **6 Calla Lily** Benjamin Moore Green Essence 853; Francesca's Paints Mint II **7Jute** Benjamin Moore Winds Breath OC-24; Fine Paints of Europe JL3 **8 String** Benjamin Moore Balboa Mist OC-27; Farrow & Ball Skimming Stone 241 **9 Oatmeal** Benjamin Moore Collingwood OC-28; Francesca's Paints The MIST **10 Natural Canvas** Benjamin Moore Silver Satin OC-26; Fine Paints of Europe JL2 **11 Bone** Benjamin Moore Classic Gray OC-23; Fine Paints of Europe SK-10 **12 Mimosa** Benjamin Moore Cloud Cover OC-25; Farrow & Ball Strong White 2001

PAGE 174 BUTTERMILK
1 Papyrus Benjamin Moore Antique White 909; Farrow & Ball Ringwold Ground 208 **2 Curd** Benjamin Moore Pelican Beach 908; Farrow Ball New White 59 **3 Cow's Milk** Benjamin Moore Evening White 907; Francesca's Paints Atone **4 Popcorn** Benjamin Moore White Mountains 906; Francesca's Paint Christophe's White **5 Lily of the Valley** Benjamin Moore Lily of the Valley 905; Francesca's Paints Sand I **6 Vanilla** Benjamin Moore White Blush 904; Farrow & Ball White Tie 2002 **7 Crème Brûlée** Benjamin Moore Love Always 896; Farrow & Ball Pink Ground 202 **8 Sesame Seed** Benjamin Moore Aphrodite Pink 895; Paint & Paper Library Coral ! **9 Salmon White** Benjamin Moore Sheer Pink 894; Paint & Paper Library Coral I **10 Ambrosia** Benjamin Moore Ambrosia 893; Sherwin-Williams 6323 Romance **11 Warm Blush** Benjamin Moore Warm Blush 892; Fine Paints of Europe SK-1 **12 Butter Churn** Benjamin Moore Opal 891; Fine Paints of Europe SK-2

PAGE 175 BISCOTTI
1 Barley Benjamin Moore Pale Moon OC-108; Francesca's Paint Boiled Egg II **2 Natural Calico** Benjamin Moore Antique Lace OC-104, Francesca's Paint Cream **3 Shortcake** Benjamin Moore Goldtone OC-112; Francesca's Paints Mascarpone **4 Cornish Cream** Benjamin Moore Man on the Moon OC-106; Farrow & Ball House White 2012 **5 White Truffle** Benjamin Moore Powder Sand OC-113; Sherwin-Williams 0051 Classic Ivory **6 Dairy Milk** Benjamin Moore Lemon Chiffon OC-109; Francesca's Paints Poppy Cream **7 Parchment** Benjamin Moore Antique Parchment 959: Paint & Paper Library Paper IV **8 Café Latte** Benjamin Moore Ocean Beach 958; Sherwin-Williams 0010 Wickerwork **9 Cashmere** Benjamin Moore Papaya 957; Farrow & Ball String 8 **10 Bleached Beech** Benjamin Moore Palace White 956; Francesca's Paints Moonlight **11 Oat Cake** Benjamin Moore Berber White 955; Paint & Paper Library Suede III **12 Limewash** Benjamin Moore Spring in Aspen 954; Paint & Paper Library Suede 1

PAGE 178 SPRING COLORS
1 Clotted Cream Benjamin Moore Timid White OC-39; Sherwin-Williams 6421 Celery **2 Chalk Pit** Benjamin Moore Litchfield Gray HC-78; Sherwin-Williams 7723 Colony Buff **3 Pewter** Benjamin Moore Silent Night 1613; Sherwin-Williams 7655 Stamped Concrete **4 Yellow Flower** Benjamin Moore Yellow Lotus 2021-50; Sherwin-Williams 6909 Lemon Twist **5 Billowy Down** Benjamin Moore Billowy Down 2064-70; Sherwin-Williams 6960 Bewitching Blue **6 Cactus Flower** Benjamin Moore Cactus Flower 1335; Sherwin-Wlliams 6600 Enticing Red

PAGE 179 LILAC LINEN
1 Alabaster Benjamin Moore White Ice OC-58; Francesca's Paints Pavilion **2 Clotted Cream** Benjamin Moore Timid White OC-39; Sherwin-Williams 6421 Celery **3 Beige Sand** Benjamin Moore Shabby Chic 1018; Sherwin-Williams 7712 Townhouse Tan **4 Lavender Blue** Benjamin Moore Snugglepuss 1405; Sherwin-Williams 6551 Purple Passage **5 Wild Orchid** Benjamin Moore Wild Orchid 2072-40; Sherwin-Williams 6832 Impulsive Purple **6 Exotic Red** Benjamin Moore Exotic Red 2086-10; Sherwin-Williams 6866 Heartthrob

PAGE 182 STRAWBERRIES & CREAM
1 Curd Benjamin Moore Pelican Beach 908; Farrow Ball New White 59 **2 Winter Snow** Benjamin Moore Winter Snow OC-63; Sherwin-Williams 7005 Pure White **3 Dark Oak** Benjamin Moore Fox Run 1229; Sherwin-Williams 6110 Steady Brown **4 Deep Rose** Benjamin Moore Deep Rose 2004-10; Sherwin-Williams 6321 Red Bay **5 Mauve Mist** Benjamin Moore Mauve Mist 1264; Sherwin-Williams 6053 Reddened Earth **6 Mauve Sable** Francesca's Paints Mud; Benjamin Moore Wooded Vista 1162

PAGE 183 BUTTERCUP & MOLE
1 Lily of the Valley Benjamin Moore Lily of the Valley 905; Francesca's Paints Sand I **2 Stoneground** Benjamin Moore Traditional Yellow, Farrow & Ball Farrow's Cream 67 **3 Allspice** Benjamin Moore Caramel Corn 2160-10; Sherwin-Williams 6370 Saucy Gold **4 Blueberry** Benjamin Moore Blueberry 2063-30; Sherwin-Williams 6524 Commodore **5 Paper White** Benjamin Moore Paper White OC-55; Francesca's Paint French Gray **6 French Horn** Benjamin Moore French Horn 195; Sherwin-Williams 6671 Curry

PAGE 186 CAPPUCCINO SCREEN
1 Parchment Benjamin Moore Antique Parchment 959; Paint & Paper Library Paper IV **2 Golden Wheat** Benjamin Moore Bryant Gold HC-7; Sherwin-Williams 6383 Golden Rule **3 Green Pearl** Benjamin Moore Sweet Spring 1500; Francesca's Paints Calm Green **4 Field Green** Benjamin Moore Waterbury Green HC-136; Sherwin-Williams 6461 Isle of Pines **5 Mocha Express** Benjamin Moore Whitall Brown HC-69; Sherwin-Williams 7055 Enduring Bronze **6 Pale Primrose** Benjamin Moore Lemon Grass 339; Sherwin-Williams 6909 Lemon Twist

PAGE 187 FADE TO GRAY
1 White Truffle Benjamin Moore Powder Sand OC-113; Sherwin-Williams 0051 Classic Ivory **2 Cornish Cream** Benjamin Moore Man on the Moon OC-106; Farrow & Ball House White 2012 **1 Barley** Benjamin Moore Pale Moon OC-108; Francesca's Paint Boiled Egg II **4 Mauve Sand** Benjamin Moore Hint of Violet 2114-60; Sherwin-Williams 6051 Sashay Sand **5 Espresso Bean** Benjamin Moore Desert Shadows 2114-30; Sherwin-Williams 6006 Black Bean **6 Purple Taupe** Benjamin Moore Wet Concrete 2114-40; Sherwin-Williams 7509 Tiki Hut

Page 187 FIELDS OF BARLEY
1 Bleached Beech Benjamin Moore Palace White 956; Francesca's Paints Moonlight **2 Parchment** Benjamin Moore Antique Parchment 959; Paint & Paper Library Paper IV **3 Ocher** Benjamin Moore Roasted Sesame Seed 2160-40; Sherwin-Williams 6360 Folksy Gold **4 Popcorn** Benjamin Moore White Mountains 906; Francesca's Paint Christophe's White **5 Winchester Sage** Benjamin Moore Winchester Sage 628; Sherwin-Williams 6459 Judite **6 Caramel Latte** Benjamin Moore Butte Rock AC-8 ; Sherwin-Williams 7522 Meadowlark

Resources

ARCHITECTS AND DESIGNERS

1100 Architect
New York
Tel: + 1 212 645 1011
www.1100architect.com

Abraham & Thakore Ltd.
New Delhi, India
Tel: + 91 11 699 3714
www.abrahamandthakore.com

Karim el Achak Architects
Marrakesh, Morocco
Tel:+ 212 24 44 73 13

Jenny Armit
London Tel: + 44 (0) 20 7792 2121
Los Angeles Tel: + 1 310 659 5261
www.jennyarmit.com

Paolo Badesco
Milan, Italy
Tel:+ 39 (0) 24 100737
www.paolobadesco.it

Linda Barker
London, U.K.
Tel: + 44 (0) 845 330 2880
www.reallylindabarker.co.uk

John Barman
New York
Tel:+ 1 212 838 9443
www.johnbarman.com

Solis Betancourt
Washington, D.C.
Tel:+ 1 202 659 8734
www.solisbetancourt.com

Jeffrey Bilhuber
Bilhuber & Associates, New York
Tel:+ 1 212 308 4888
www.bilhuber.com

Sonja and John Caproni
Caproni Associates, New York
Tel:+ 1 212 977 4010

Alexandra Champalimaud & Associates
New York
Tel: + 1 212 807 8869
www.alexchamp.com

Jane Churchill
London, U.K.
Tel: + 44 (0)20 7244 7427
www.janechurchill.com

Clodagh Design
New York
Tel: + 1 212 780 5755
www.clodagh.com

David Collins Architecture and Design
London, U.K.
Tel: +44 (0) 20 7835 5000
www.davidcollins.com

Coorengel & Calvagrac
Paris, France
Tel:+ 33 1 40 27 14 65
www.coorengel-calvagrac.com

Agnès Comar
Paris, France
Tel:+ 33 1 47 23 33 85

Bernie de Le Cuona
London, U.K.
Tel: + 44 (0)20 7584 7677
www.delecuona.co.uk

Jamie Drake
New York
Tel:+ 1 212 754 3099
www.drakedesignassociates.com

Agnès Emery
Brussels Tel:+ 32 2 513 5892
London Tel: c/o Retrouvius + 44 (0) 20 8969 0222
www.emeryetcie.com

Luigi Esposito
London, U.K.
Tel: + 44 (0)20 7584 9495
www.casaforma.co.uk

Ramón Esteve Architects
Valencia, Spain
Tel:+ 34 96 351 04 34
www.ramonesteve.com

Frank Faulkner
Catskill, New York
Tel:+ 1 518 943 9220
www.frankfaulkner.com

Patrizio Fradiani
Studio F, Chicago, Illinois
Tel:+ 1 773 880 0450
www.studiof-design.com

Anne Fougeron
San Francisco, CA
Tel:+ 1 415 641 5744
www.fougeron.com

Karl Fournier and Olivier Marty
Studio KO, Paris, France & Marrakesh, Morocco
Paris Tel:+ 33 1 42 71 13 92
www.studioko.fr

Christophe Gollut
London, U.K.
Tel: +44 (0) 20 7370 4021

Philip Gorrivan Design
New York
Tel: + 1 212 339 7696
www.philipgorrivan.com

Johnny Grey
Hampshire, U.K Tel:+44 1730 821424
Mount Clemens, MI Tel: + 1 888 902 8860
www.johnnygrey.com

John Hobby
Space, Atlanta, Georgia
Tel:+ 1 404 228 4600
www.spacemodern.com

Dominique Kieffer
Paris Tel:+ 33 1 56 81 20 20
London Tel: +44 (0) 7349 1590
www.dkieffer.com

Hilton McConnico
Bagnolet, France
Tel: + 33 143 625 316
www.hiltonmcconnico.com

Ilaria Miani
Rome, Italy
Tel:+ 39 06 6833160
www.ilariamiani.it

John Minshaw Designs Ltd.
London, U.K.
Tel: +44 (0) 20 7486 5777
www.johnminshawdesigns.com

Mimmi O'Connell
London, U.K.
Tel: +44 (0) 20 7752 0474
www.mimmioconnell.com

John Pardey Architects
Hampshire, U.K.
Tel: + 44 (0) 1590 626465
www.johnpardeyarchitects.com

Paul + O Architects
London, U.K.
Tel: +44 (0) 20 7604 3818
www.paul-o-architects.com

Guy Peterson/Ofa
Sarasota, Florida
Tel: + 1 941 952 1111
www.guypeterson.com

Lena Proudlock
Denim in Style, Tetbury, U.K.
Tel: +44 (0) 1666 50051
www.lenaproudlock.com

Karim Rashid
New York
Tel: + 1 212 929 8656
www.karimrashid.com

Jonathan Reed
Studio Reed, London, U.K.
Tel: +44 (0) 20 7565 0066

Johann Slee
Stellenbosch, South Africa
Tel:+ 27 21 887 3385
www.slee.co.za

Rupert Spira
U.K.
Tel: +44 (0) 1588 650588
www.rupertspira.com

Philippe Stark
Paris, France
Tel:+ 33 1 48 07 54 54
www.stark.com

John Stefanidis
London, U.K.
Tel: +44 (0) 20 7808 4700
www.johnstefanidis.com

Axel Vervoordt
Gravenwezel, Belgium
Tel:+ 32 658 1470
www.axel-vervoordt.com

Nicolas Vignot
Paris, France
Tel: + 33 6 11 96 67 69
http://n.vignot.free.fr

Peter Wadley Architects
London, U.K.
Tel: +44 (0) 20 8747 8833
www.wadleyarchitects.com

John Wardle Architects
Melbourne, Victoria, Australia
Tel: + 61 39 6548700
www.johnwardle.com

Donald A. Wexler Associates
California
Tel: + 1 760 320 1709

SHOPS

ABC Carpet & Home
New York
Tel: + 1 212 473 3000
www.abchome.com

GP & J Baker
London, UK
Tel: + 44 (0) 20 7351 7760
www.gpjbaker.com

Solgården
Stockholm, Sweden
Tel: + 46 8 663 9360
www.solgarden.net

Traditions
New York
Tel: + 1 518 851 3975

PAINT SUPPLIERS

Auro Natural Paints
Cheltenham Road
Bisley, Nr Stroud
Gloucestershire GL6 7BX, U.K.
Tel: +44 (0) 1452 772020
www.auro.co.uk

Behr Paints
3400 W Segerstrom Ave
Santa Ana, CA 92704
Tel: + 1 714 545 7101
www.behr.com

Benjamin Moore & Co.
101 Paragon Drive
Montvale, NJ 07645
Tel: + 1 800 344 0400
www.benjaminmoore.com

Calico Corners
Customer Service, 203 Gale Lane
Kennett Square, PA 19348
Tel: + 1 800 213 6366
www.calicocorners.com

Craig & Rose
Unit 8, Halbeath Industrial Estate,
Dunfermline, Fife KY11 7EG, U.K.
Tel: + 44 (0) 1254 704951
www.craigandrose.com

Crown Paints
Hollins Road
Darwen BB3 OBG, U.K.
Tel: + 44 (0) 870 240 1127
www.crownpaint.co.uk

Dulux Paints
Slough, U.K.
Tel: + 44 (0) 870 444 11 11
www.dulux.co.uk

Ecos Organic Paints
Unit 19, Heysham Business Park
Middleton Road, Heysham
Lancs LA3 3PP, U.K.
Tel: +44 (0) 1524 852371
www.ecospaints.com

Farrow & Ball
Uddens Estate, Wimborne
Dorset BH21 7NL, U.K.
Tel: +44 (0) 1202 876141
www.farrow-ball.com

Fine Paints of Europe
P O Box 419
Woodstock, VT 05091
Tel: + 1 800 332 1556
www.finepaintsofeurope.com

Fired Earth Interiors
3 Twyford Mill, Oxford Road,
Adderbury, Nr Banbury
Oxfordshire OX17 3SX, U.K.
Tel: + 44 (0) 1295 812088
www.firedearth.com

Flamant
The Original Paint Collection
p/a Dendermondsesteenweg 75
B-9300 Aalst, Belgium
Tel: + 32 (0) 53 76 80 21
www.flamantpaint.com

Francesca's Paints
Unit 34, Battersea Business Centre
99/109 Lavender Hill
London SW11 5QL, U.K.
Tel: + 44 (0) 20 7228 7694
www.francescaspaint.com

The Freshaire Choice Paints
Tel: + 1 866 880 0304
www.thefreshairechoice@ici.com
No-VOC paint from ICI available at Home Depot

Glidden
ICI Paints
Cleveland, Ohio
Tel: + 1 800 454 3336
www.glidden.com

Home Depot
Tel: + 1 800 553 3199
www.homedepot.com

Kelly Hoppen Interiors
2 Munden Street
London W14 ORH, U.K.
Tel: + 44 (0) 20 747 3350
www.kellyhoppen.com

ICI Paints
Slough, U.K.
Tel: + 44 (0) 870 444 11 11
www.dulux.co.uk

Ralph Lauren Paint
Tel: + 1 800 379 POLO
www.ralphlaurenhome.com

Leyland Paints
Tel: +44 (0) 1924 354600
www.leyland-paints.co.uk

The Little Greene Paint Company
Wood Street, Openshaw,
Manchester M11 2FB, U.K.
Tel: +44 (0) 161 2300 880
www.thelittlegreene.com

Marston & Langinger
192 Ebury Street
London SW1W 8UP, U.K.
Tel: +44 (0) 20 7881 5710
www.marston-and-langinger.com

Nordic Style
109 Lots Road
London SW10 020, U.K.
Tel: + 44 (0) 20 7451 1753
www.nordicstyle.biz

Nutshell Natural Paints
Unit 3, Leigham Units
Silverton Road, Matford Park
Exeter, Devon, EX2 8HY, U.K.
Tel: + 44 (0) 1392 823760
www.nutshellpaints.com

Old Village Paint
P O Box 130
Perkiomenville, PA 18074
Tel: + 1 800 498 7687
www.old-village.com

The Paint & Paper Library
5 Elystan Street
London SW3 3NT, U.K.
Tel: + 44 (0) 20 7823 7755
www.paintlibrary.co.uk

Papers and Paints
4 Park Walk
London SW10 0AD, U.K.
Tel: + 44 (0) 20 7352 8626
www.papers-paints.co.uk

Plascon Paints
South Africa
Tel: + 27 (0) 860 204060
www.plascon.co.za

Porter's Paints
895 Bourke St
Waterloo, Sydney
NSW 2017, Australia
www.porterspaints.com.au
Tel: + 61 (0) 2 9698 5322

Restoration Hardware
2900 North MacArthur Drive
Suite 100
Tracy, CA 95376
Tel: + 1 800 910 9836
www.restorationhardwarc.com

Sherwin-Williams
Tel: + 1 800 832 2541
www.sherwin-williams.com

Annie Sloan Paints
117 London Road, Headington
Oxford, Oxon OX3 9HZ
Tel: + 44 (0) 1865 768666
www.anniesloan.com

Martha Stewart Colors
Tel: + 1 888 562 7842
www.marthastewart.com
Available only at Lowe's USA

Sun Wallpaper & Paint
47 Overocker Road
Poughkeepsie, NY 12603
Tel: + 1 845 471 2880
www.sunwallpaperandpaint.com

Acknowledgments

No book of this sort could ever achieve perfection without the assistance of many specialist paint producers, color experts, and designers. Once again I find I have had the very generous assistance of many friends and colleagues who have given their valuable time to guide me through the maze of color available to us today.

Francesca Wezel—my friend, colleague, and valued advisor—once again stepped in and talked me through every color under the sun with her usual vigor, excitement, talent, and inspiration. Whether she was explaining to me how bathrooms should always be painted pink as it is the most flattering color, or helping me find the perfect off-white, she never lost patience or originality. Nor did she ever make me feel I was a nuisance—and I am sure I was. An enormous thank you to Francesca on my behalf and on yours, too, dear reader!

Thank you, David Oliver, for teaching us how to see the light by viewing the color on different sides of the room by using a shoe box. Thank you Luigi Esposito, Vicente Wolf, Jamie Drake, and Agnès Emery for your professional secrets on creating wonderful living spaces—all different and all fascinating.

Kit Kemp, legendary hotel designer, gave us hints as to the use of color that must appeal to multiple people.

Alex Bates, the Creative Director of West Elm, gave us wonderful color advice, both personal and professional, for which I am so grateful.

Photo credits

Every effort has been made to trace the copyright holders, architects, and designers. We apologize in advance for any unintentional omission, and would be pleased to insert the appropriate acknowledgment in any subsequent edition.

Location/Designer or Architect/Photographer/Agency

1 Andrea Gobbi/Simon Upton/The Interior Archive, 2 Paolo Badesco's villa in Italy/Andrew Wood, 4 Abraham & Thakore/Andrew Wood, 6 an apartment in Paris, designed by Hilton McConnico/Simon Upton, 9 above left The Hotelito in Mexico/Jenny Armit/Simon Upton; 9 above right a house in Marrakesh, designed by Karl Fournier and Olivier Marty/Studio KO/Andrew Wood, 9 below right Ulla Hagar Tornos/Fritz von der Schulenburg/The Interior Archive, 9 below left Lena Proudlock of Denim In Style's house in Gloucestershire/Simon Upton, 12 above Jamie Drake/Fritz von der Schulenburg, 12 below a house in Marrakesh, designed by Karl Fournier and Olivier Marty/Studio KO/Andrew Wood, 13 above left Jane Churchill/Simon Upton, 13 above right Simon Upton, 13 below right Shane/Cooper Residence in New York/1100 Architects/Andrew Wood, 13 below left Jane Churchill/Simon Upton, 14 above left a house in Balnarring in Coastal Victoria/John Wardle Architects/Andrew Wood, 14 above right Denis Blais (Vingt Douze)/Luke White/The Interior Archive. 15 left Susanne Boyd/Simon Upton/The Interior Archive, 15 right Jane Churchill/Simon Upton, 16 above left Hilton McConnico's house in Paris/Simon Upton, 16 above right Jamie Drake's apartment in New York/Andrew Wood, 16 below right Philip Gorrivan/Simon Upton/The Interior Archive, 16 below left Johnny Grey/Alex Wilson, 17 Jane Churchill/Simon Upton, 18 left Linda Barker/Lucinda Symons, 18 right a house in the Hamptons, designed by Solis Betancourt/Simon Upton, 19 Linda Barker/Lucinda Symons, 25 above left The Hotelito in Mexico/Jenny Armit/Simon Upton, 25 above right Philippe Stark/Simon Upton/The Interior Archive, 25 below right Eric and Gloria Stewart's manor house in southwestern France /Simon Upton, 25 below left Peter Wadley/Tim Beddow/The Interior Archive, 26 Ilaria Miani/Simon Upton, 28 Jane Churchill/Simon Upton, 29 Armand Ventilo/Mark Luscombe-Whyte/The Interior Archive, 30 left Jane Churchill/Simon Upton, 30 right Linda Barker/Lucinda Symons, 31 Jane Churchill/Simon Upton, 32 Richard Mudditt/Fritz von der Schulenburg/The Interior Archive, 33 Jane Churchill/Simon Upton, 34 Jane Churchill/Simon Upton, 35 Mary Drysdale's house in Pennsylvania/Andrew Wood, 36 John Stefanidis/Fritz von der Schulenburg/The Interior Archive, 37 Manolo Mestre/Mark Luscombe-Whyte/The Interior Archive, 38 Jamie Drake/Fritz von der Schulenberg, 39 Alex Possenbacher/Mark Luscombe-Whyte/The Interior Archive, 45 above left Rupert Spira/Simon Upton, 45 above right Karim Rashid/Andrew Wood, 45 below The Hotelito in Mexico/Jenny Armit/Simon Upton, 46 Jane Churchill/Simon Upton, 48 Ali Sharland's house in Gloucestershire/Simon Upton, 49 Shane/Cooper Residence in New York/1100 Architects/Andrew Wood, 50 Christophe Gollut's house in Gran Canaria/Simon Upton, 51 Agnès Comar/Fritz von der Schulenberg, 52 John Pardey/Mark Luscombe-Whyte/The Interior Archive, 53 Andrew Allfree/Simon Upton/The Interior Archive, 54 Designer: Jim Isermann; Architect: Donald Wexler/Mark Luscombe-Whyte/The Interior Archive, 55 Francoise Smilenko/Vincent Knapp/The Interior Archive, 56 Charles de Sellier's house in Brussels/Simon Upton, 57 Lincoln/Orum Residence in Suffolk/Angi Lincoln/Andrew Wood, 58 Abraham & Thakore/Andrew Wood, 59 left Karim el Achak's house in Marrakesh/Andrew Wood, 59 right Karim el Achak's house in Marrakesh/Andrew Wood, 65 above left Luke White, 65 above right The Hotelito in Mexico/Jenny Armit/Simon Upton, 65 below Jenny Armit/Simon Upton, 67 Michael Coorengel & Jean-Pierre Calvagrac/Fritz von der Schulenberg, 68 Nicholas Alvis Vega and Liza Bruce/Simon Upton/The Interior Archive, 69 an apartment in Paris, designed by Hilton McConnico/Simon Upton, 70 left Fishman Residence in Florida/Don Chapell/Andrew Wood, 70 right Lynne Forneles of Febo Design/Andrew Wood, 71 Fishman Residence in Florida/Don Chapell/Andrew Wood, 72 Nathalie Lete/Frederic Vasseur/The Interior Archive, 73-74 Jenny Armit/Simon Upton, 75 Jamie Drake's apartment in New York/Simon Upton, 76 Nathalie Lete/Frederic Vasseur/The Interior Archive, 77 Karim el Achak's house in Marrackech/Andrew Wood, 78 Michael Coorengel & Jean-Pierre Calvagrac/Fritz von der Schulenberg, 79 Nathalie Lete/Frederic Vasseur/The Interior Archive, 85 above left Fishman Residence in Florida/Don Chapell/Andrew Wood, 85 above right Agnès Emery's house in Marrakesh/Simon Upton, 85 below right Andrea Gobbi/Simon Upton/The Interior Archive, 85 below left Carlos Mota (Miles Redd)/Simon Upton/The Interior

Archive, 86 Jane Churchill/Simon Upton, 88 Jane Churchill/Simon Upton, 89 Hilton McConnico/Simon Upton, 90 left Graham Head (of ABC Carpet & Home) and Barbara Rathbourne's house in Long Island/Andrew Wood, 90 right Barbara Kurgan and James Andrew/Simon Upton/The Interior Archive, 91 Jane Churchill/Simon Upton, 92 Jane Churchill/Simon Upton, 93 Jane Churchill/Simon Upton, 94 Neilama Residence, Helsinki/Ulla Koskinen/Andrew Wood, 95 Agnès Emery's house in Marrakesh/Simon Upton, 96 a house in Ibiza, designed by Ramón Esteve Architects/Andrew Wood, 97 Linda Barker/Lucinda Symons, 98 John Minshaw Designs Ltd./Simon Upton/The Interior Archive, 99 a riverside apartment in London, designed by Luigi Esposito/Luke White, 100 Elena and Stephen Georgiadis' house in London/John Minshaw Designs Ltd./Simon Upton, 101 left Agnès Emery's house in Marrakesh/Simon Upton, 101 right Axel Vervoordt's house in Belgium/Simon Upton, 107 above left Agnès Emery's house in Marrakesh/Simon Upton, 107 above right Penny Morrison/Tim Beddow/The Interior Archive, 107 below Paul + O Architects/Mark Luscombe-Whyte/The Interior Archive, 108 Julie Prisca's house in Normandy/Simon Upton, 110 George Residence, extension and remodelling/Michael George/Andrew Wood, 111 Jane Churchill/Simon Upton, 112 left Lynn von Kersting/Andrew Wood, 112 right Peri Wolfman and Charles Gold's house in Bridgehampton/Simon Upton, 113 Jane Churchill/Simon Upton, 114 Pamela Kline (of Traditions)'s house in Claverack, New York/Simon Upton, 115 Jane Churchill/Simon Upton, 116 Jane Churchill/Simon Upton, 117 Mark Luscombe-Whyte/The Interior Archive, 118 a house in Connecticut, designed by Jeffrey Bilhuber/Simon Upton, 119 Shane/Cooper Residence in New York/1100 Architects/Andrew Wood, 120 David Collins Architecture and Design/Fritz von der Schulenberg, 121 left David Carter/Simon Upton, 121 right Nathan Turner/Simon Upton, 127 above left Codman House, a property of the Society of the Preservation of New England Antiquities/Simon Upton, 127 above right a house in Marrakesh designed by Karl Fournier and Olivier Marty/Studio KO/Andrew Wood, 127 below right Bernie de le Cuona/Simon Upton, 127 below left a house in London, designed by Jonathan Reed/Simon Upton, 130 Carlos Mota and Miles Redd/Simon Upton/The Interior Archive, 131 Jamie Drake/Fritz von der Schulenberg, 132 a penthouse in New York, designed by Clodagh Design/Luke White, 133 left Andrew Wood 133 right Ianthe Ruthven/The Interior Archive, 134 & 135 a house in Marrakesh, designed by Karl Fournier & Olivier Marty/Studio KO/Andrew Wood, 136 & 137 Johann Slee's house in Johannesburg/Andrew Wood, 138 Jeffrey Bilhuber/Simon Upton, 139 Virginia Fisher/Fritz von Schulenburg/The Interior Archive, 140 a house in London by Jonathan Reed/Simon Upton, 141 an apartment in Paris, designed by Hilton McConnico/Simon Upton, 142 Bernie de Le Cuona/Luke White, 143 Ilaria Miani/Simon Upton, 144 Philip Gorrivan/Simon Upton/The Interior Archive, 145 Patrick Gwynne/Tim Beddow/the Interior Archive, 151 above left Axel Vervoordt/Simon Upton, 151 above right Véronique Lopez's house from Casa Lopez/Simon Upton, 151 below right Linda Barker(Towbridge Prints)/Lucinda Symons, 151 below left Dominique Kieffer's house in Normandy/Simon Upton, 153 Mimmi O'Connell/Simon Upton, 154 Jane Churchill/Simon Upton, 155 Mark Gilbey and Polly Dicken's house in Pennsylvannia/Simon Upton, 156 Vincente Wolf/Andrew Wood, 157 Jane Churchill/Simon Upton, 158 Michael Coorengel & Jean-Pierre Calvagrac's apartment in Paris/Luke White, 159–160 Linda Barker (Crown Paint)/Lucinda Symons, 161 Marianne von Kantzow's shop Solgården in Stockholm/Simon Upton, 162 Dominique Kieffer's house in Normandy/Simon Upton, 163 John Barman's apartment in New York/Simon Upton, 164 left Paolo Badesco's villa in Italy/Andrew Wood, 164 right Frank Faulkner's house in Catskill, New York/Simon Upton, 165 Alexandra Champalimaud/Simon Upton, 166 left Peri Wolfman and Charles Gold's house in Bridgehampton/Simon Upton, 166 right Dominique Kieffer's house in Normandy/Simon Upton, 167 left Kristiina Ratia's house in Connecticut/Andrew Wood, 167 right Jeffrey Bilhuber/Simon Upton, 173 above left Mannisto/Poyhonen apartment in Helsinki/Tuula Poyhonen/Andrew Wood, 173 above right Jeannette Chang's apartment in New York/Sonja & John Caproni/Simon Upton, 173 below right a house in Atlanta designed by Tim Hobby of Space/Simon Upton, 173 below left a house in Connecticut designed by Jeffrey Bilhuber/Simon Upton, 175 Jane Churchill/Simon Upton, 176 Dominique Kieffer's house in Normandy/Simon Upton, 177 Patrizio Fradiani's house in Chicago/Patrizio Fradiani at Studio F/Frederic Vasseur, 178 Graham Head (of ABC Carpet & Home) and Barbara Rathbourne's house in Long Island/Andrew Wood, 179 Jane Churchill/Simon Upton, 180 Andrew Wood , 181-183 Jane Churchill/Simon Upton, 184 Anthony Cochrane's apartment in New York/Simon Upton, 185 Jane Churchhill/Simon Upton, 186 Matthew Drennan and Hamish McArdle's house in London/Dalsouple/Lucinda Symons, 187 left a riverside apartment in London designed by Luigi Esposito/Luke White, 187 right Jane Churchill/Simon Upton

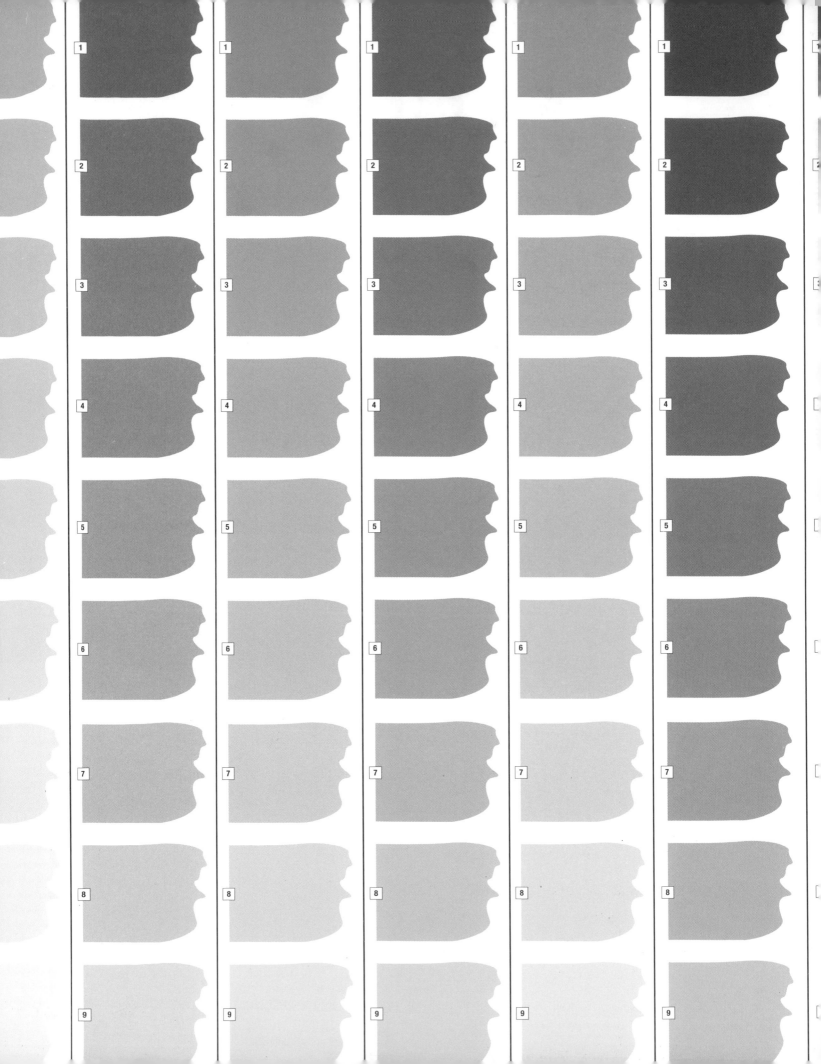